BALTIMORE
PROHIBITION

WET & DRY IN THE FREE STATE

MICHAEL T. WALSH

AMERICAN PALATE

Published by American Palate
A Division of The History Press
Charleston, SC
www.historypress.net

Front cover image courtesy of Library of Congress. Back cover brick wall image courtesy of author.

First published 2017

Manufactured in the United States

ISBN 9781625858429

Library of Congress Control Number: 2017953985

Notice: The information in this book is true and complete to the best of our knowledge. It is offered without guarantee on the part of the author or The History Press. The author and The History Press disclaim all liability in connection with the use of this book.

*To my wife, Jennifer; my daughter, Elizabeth; and my parents, John and Annette,
for all of your unconditional love and support throughout these many years. The
next few rounds are on me. Cheers!*

CONTENTS

ACKNOWLEDGEMENTS

T hank you to all of my family and friends, especially the following: Jennifer, Elizabeth, Mom, Dad, Dave, Sara, Katie, Mike, Linda, Michelle, Mugsy and Roddy—I could not have accomplished this without your enduring and unwavering support! A very special thank-you to Jenn and Elizabeth, who toured Baltimore and Maryland with me over several weekends searching for the many historical artifacts, buildings and locations that are still highly visible but often overlooked. You both made all of those "adventures" even more fun, as I was able to share my passion for the subject with you and have someone to share my excitement with when I finally found what I was looking for!

I would like to thank my thesis and dissertation mentors at the University of Maryland Baltimore County (UMBC), Dr. John W. Jeffries and the late Dr. Joseph Arnold, both of whom helped immensely in aiding my completion of my master's thesis and doctoral dissertation on Prohibition in Baltimore—without their support and expertise, this book would not have been written! Additionally, I want to acknowledge the support of that dissertation committee as well, all of whom provided ideas over many years: Thomas Pegram, Kriste Lindenmeyer, Thomas Schaller and George LaNoue.

A great deal of gratitude to all the folks at The History Press and Arcadia Publishing, especially J. Banks Smither—your assistance and patience cannot be overstated. Thank you to Hannah Cassilly for seeing real value in my work during the book proposal stage and pitching the book to The History Press publishing committee.

Much gratitude to the faculty and staff at my alma maters: Calvert Hall College High School, Loyola University Maryland and the UMBC history, political science and public policy departments. My past and present colleagues in UMBC's Office of Sponsored Programs deserve recognition for their support of this project, as do past and present members of both Whisky Train and The Agitators.

I would like to acknowledge the help and assistance of the following repositories and the individuals who work there, without whom this endeavor could not have reached completion: the Baltimore Museum of Industry, especially Matthew Shirko and Collin Molony; Marilyn Schnider at the *Baltimore Sun*; Lisa Marine at the Wisconsin Historical Society; James Singewald at the Maryland Historical Society; Megan Craynon at the Maryland State Archives; the Library of Congress; Annie McLhinney-Cochran at the McLhinney Speakeasy Museum and International Market in Havre de Grace, Maryland; the good folks at the Gunter Hotel (who provided me and my wife with a private, spur-of-the-moment tour as we were passing through Frostburg); the Albert O. Kuhn Library at UMBC; the Loyola University Maryland/University of Notre Dame Library; the Enoch Pratt Free Library; the McKeldin Library at University of Maryland College Park; and the numerous online repositories that provided primary and secondary sources for research and interpretation throughout the years.

INTRODUCTION

It started as a germ of an idea nearly two decades ago in just a small term paper. It was the spring of 2001, and as a graduate student at the University of Maryland Baltimore County (UMBC) working toward a Master of Arts degree in historical studies, I was faced with a dilemma: I needed a term paper topic for a twenty-page paper in my HIST 642: History of Baltimore class, taught by a fantastic scholar and noted Baltimore historian, Dr. Joseph Arnold. As a native and lifelong resident of Baltimore, this was my opportunity to finally devote myself to researching and writing on a local historical subject I cared greatly about.

The problem was that I wanted to research a topic that had hitherto been of little regard to historians or perhaps even neglected completely by those practitioners in the discipline. It soon became fairly evident to me that the topic worth exploring—the prohibition of alcohol in Baltimore under the Eighteenth Amendment—was ripe for scholarship. Moreover, I found it serendipitous to combine my passion for twentieth-century Baltimore history with my taste for good local Baltimore beer! In the early 2000s, there truly was a lack of scholarship on the subject of Prohibition in Baltimore. Dr. Arnold agreed with me, so much so that he suggested I should consider turning that term paper into a possible master's thesis. And that is exactly what I did in 2001–2. Then I decided to take it a few steps further, as the thesis clearly was not as comprehensive and as all-encompassing on the subject matter as I ultimately wanted it to be.

I entered the public policy doctoral program at UMBC and elected to participate in the policy history track. I used the thesis as a broad framework and basis for my doctoral dissertation, adding years of research and writing into my studies on the subject matter and really analyzing Prohibition in Baltimore and Maryland from different historical and policy perspectives. It took many years to complete, but by the end of my studies, I had successfully completed and defended a comprehensive history and study of the national policy of Prohibition in Baltimore and Maryland.

This book is a direct result of those years I spent researching and writing the thesis and dissertation.[1] In many ways, this is a more abridged and accessible version of the dissertation geared to a general history–loving audience that enjoys a great story. After all, no one has published a real comprehensive history of Maryland's and Baltimore's experience with Prohibition. This book attempts to provide just such a narrative. It's the story and the history that I've always wanted to tell about Prohibition in my hometown.

In his book *Prohibition in Washington, D.C.: How Dry We Weren't,* author Garrett Peck provided both a history and guidebook to Prohibition in the District. This book similarly attempts to provide that same function for Baltimore and Maryland. Where appropriate, I have used contemporary photos of some of the famous locations throughout the book, places that are still visible in the Baltimore landscape today. I do hope that the written word and the remaining visual evidence of a bygone era stimulate your intellectual curiosity and feasibly allow for a nice day trip or two on a quasi-trail of Prohibition throughout Baltimore and Maryland. Cheers and happy reading!

Chapter 1

PROHIBITION IN THE "FREE STATE"

Maryland, like many states in the United States, has its fair share of popular nicknames. Arguably, Maryland's most famous nickname that is still frequently articulated in the twenty-first century is the "Free State." The nickname connotes an adoration of freedom and liberty, those stalwart patriotic ideals that surely resonate with the residents of the state and thus provide a certain sense of civic pride. But one could dare say that most Marylanders today have little idea of the origins of that nickname and the true, and somewhat subversive, meaning behind that now-iconic state moniker.

The coining of Maryland as the "Free State" is credited to *Baltimore Evening Sun* editor Hamilton Owens, who bestowed that nickname in 1922.[2] Why was Owens driven to develop this new nickname for his home state? He was an eyewitness to his state's outright defiance of the Eighteenth Amendment, the constitutional amendment that prohibited the sale, transportation and distribution of alcohol in the United States. The amendment led to national Prohibition (with a capital *P*), a federal law that was theoretically in effect from 1920 through 1933. In 1922, Owens created that name to describe Maryland's ultimate act of rebellion against that amendment, as the Maryland state legislature refused to pass any state enforcement act—what was termed a "baby Volstead"—for Prohibition. Maryland became the *only* state in the Union to not pass such legislation. Thus, Maryland truly was the "Free State."

A great deal has been published on Prohibition, especially during the past sixty years. One of the most controversial policies ever enacted in the United States, Prohibition was perhaps the most visible and publicized issue from the late nineteenth century until its repeal in 1933.[3] Historian Allan J. Lichtman has stated that "more than any other policy issue of the 1920s, Prohibition commanded public interest and attention."[4] As the decades have passed, literature on Prohibition has proliferated as historians and social scientists have examined the subject matter in macro/national studies, as well as specific case studies. Thus, the study of and public interest in the topic of Prohibition certainly is well deserved.

Major metropolitan cities and regions such as New York, Detroit, Chicago and Washington, D.C., as well as more rural states like Kansas and Montana, have received a great deal of attention from professional historians, filmmakers and the everyday history buff who have a keen interest in all things Prohibition.[5] Nonetheless, the Prohibition era in one major city and state located on the East Coast—one of the original thirteen colonies, no less—has not been substantially studied and rigorously published over the years. It is tremendously surprising in many ways that the story of Prohibition in Baltimore and Maryland has not been satisfactorily articulated in any real comprehensive manner.

In fact, the importance of Baltimore and Maryland during the reign of Prohibition has been largely ignored by even those historians who study Prohibition at the national/macro level. Yet both Baltimore and Maryland had a significant and influential role in the enactment of, response to and termination of the policy of national Prohibition, and the stories, anecdotes and available data are all important and instructive in gauging the impact of the national Prohibition policy on society, culture and politics.

In some locales, the enactment and attempted enforcement of Prohibition produced a highly volatile environment.[6] Such was the case in Baltimore and Maryland, as urban wets and rural drys constantly battled each other with words, and sometimes fists, in the fight over Prohibition. The primary focus of this book is the city of Baltimore. However, the story in the rest of the state of Maryland is integral to understanding the experiences of the city. Baltimore was viewed as a "center of resistance to prohibition," a thoroughly wet city with a diverse population, while many other Maryland counties, though less populated, tended to favor dry laws.[7]

The fact that large parts of Maryland were dry had an effect on Baltimore's actions and reactions to the implementation of Prohibition and its subsequent enforcement. Nevertheless, perhaps the fundamental reason for why the emphasis of this book is placed on Baltimore is the sheer size of its population in relation to the rest of the state. Baltimore was one of the largest cities in the United States during this era, easily the largest city south of the Mason-Dixon line (New Orleans's population was at least 200,000 less than Baltimore's).[8] Roughly half of Maryland's total population lived in Baltimore City during the only full decade of Prohibition. The 1920 census shows that Maryland's total population was 1,449,661 persons,[9] with 733,826 residing in Baltimore City. The 1930 census shows that there was a total population of 1,631,526 persons in Maryland, while Baltimore City's population consisted of 804,874 persons.[10] Moreover, the highest county population in the state in 1920 and 1930 (74,817 persons and 124,565 persons, respectively) belonged to Baltimore County, whose boundaries abutted those of the city and which was the only Maryland county to join Baltimore City in not having a local option law—a law in which the local legislature or political unit would decide whether or not to sell licenses for liquor to be sold within a stated specified boundary—before 1920.[11]

This 1927 photo presents a view of the Central Business District of Baltimore from Broadway. *Baltimore Museum of Industry, Baltimore Gas & Electric Company Photographic Collection, BGE.3209N.*

A 1942 map of Baltimore City and its immediate surrounding counties. The map shows the city boundaries as they would have appeared from 1918 to 1933. *Baltimore Museum of Industry, Baltimore Gas & Electric Company Photographic Collection, BGE.14908.*

Baltimore's significant population in relation to the state of Maryland also affected its political relevance and power in Annapolis. Maryland's General Assembly is a bicameral legislative body consisting of the Maryland Senate and the House of Delegates. During the period under study, whereas Baltimore County's representation in the state's legislative body remained unchanged (1 senator and 6 delegates), Baltimore City's representation did change and, in fact, increased. From 1913 through 1922, there was a total of 27 state senators (4 from Baltimore—1 each from Baltimore's four districts) and 102 delegates (24 from Baltimore—6 from each of Baltimore's four districts).[12] The 1918 annexation that increased Baltimore's boundaries from thirty square miles to its current ninety-two square miles increased Baltimore's population by about 200,000 persons and therefore necessitated a need for a greater representation from Baltimore in the assembly. In 1922, an amendment to the Maryland Constitution was passed that granted Baltimore City two more districts, increasing Baltimore's number of senators from 4 to 6 and its delegates from 24 to 36. Baltimore City's influence on Maryland politics, thus, increased rather dramatically during the Prohibition era.

If one could envision the policy of Prohibition as an ensemble stage play, Baltimore and Maryland would have one of the leading and starring roles, essential to the ongoing narrative of the story and at least partially responsible for the entertaining climax. The story of Prohibition in Baltimore and Maryland provides a glimpse into the not-so-long-ago past, when clandestine speakeasies replaced the city's saloons and breweries; "wets" and "drys" battled vociferously with each other in the press, courts and government arena; spiritual and community leaders took center stage in debates over policy; and bootleggers and rumrunners became cult heroes despite an alleged increase in crime. For thirteen years, Prohibition was the law of the land, and Baltimore and Maryland were prime battlegrounds between the supporters and opponents of what may very well be the most provocative law ever implemented.

Chapter 2

"CLOSING TIME!"

The Enactment of Prohibition

Formulating and implementing a national law as complex as Prohibition took time. If it was to be successful, it had to be done correctly. For the supporters of a national Prohibition policy, often collectively referred to as "drys," they had years of past legislation and prior experience they could utilize in order to develop a solid constitutional law. Thus, prohibiting the manufacture and distribution of alcoholic beverages across all the states was neither a radical nor a spontaneous policy decision. The advent of national Prohibition in 1920 was actually the culmination of a decades-long, incremental approach to achieving a more temperate society in America. And Baltimore and Maryland had starring roles in that buildup toward national Prohibition.

Calls for temperance had sufficiently permeated the very fabric of American social and political life in the mid- to late nineteenth century. But even well before that period, there are examples of laws that were constructed to punish those who were intemperate and publicly inebriated. For example, during the colonial period in 1642, Maryland punished drunkenness with a fine of one hundred pounds of tobaccos.[13] Additionally, Maryland colonial records of laws suggesting the need for some sort of prohibition or control of alcohol can be found at least as far back as 1688, when it was suggested by Tom Calvert, the king of one of the Indian tribes.[14]

Perhaps it is therefore not a surprise that Baltimore and Maryland also played a major role in the generation of prohibition policies that directly preceded the adoption of the Eighteenth Amendment. The modern

American experience with the notion of a prohibition policy of any kind has generally been recognized to begin with the Washington Temperance Society, which was formed at Baltimore's own Chase's Tavern on Liberty Street on April 2, 1840, by six reformed drinkers (William Mitchell, David Hoss, Charles Anderson, George Steer, Bill M'Curdy and Tom Campbell).[15] Typically, such societies called for temperance, not necessarily prohibition. The Washingtonian movement proved to be pioneering because it included men, women, merchants, unskilled laborers and artisans alike.[16] This unique quality helped the organization to spread rapidly in Baltimore and expand into other cities such as New York, Boston and Cincinnati.[17] However, support for the Washingtonians dwindled in the following years as critics chastised the organization for a lack of religious foundation and an informal organizational structure.[18]

In 1850s Baltimore, the rise of the Know Nothing Party and its subsequent attempts at reforming liquor laws (based on the often-correct belief that the saloons frequently corrupted politics and heavily influenced the outcome of elections, as well as based on the party's anti-immigrant views) gave birth to a subset known as the Friends of the Maine Liquor Law.[19] The Maine Liquor Law comprised numerous bills passed between 1846 and 1851 that prohibited the sale of intoxicating beverages, except for medicinal and/or industrial purposes, in Maine.[20] In 1853, the Friends of the Maine Liquor Law group in Baltimore was able to elect ten delegates to the Maryland General Assembly on a platform that "denounced the manufacture, sale, and consumption of intoxicating liquors."[21] During the General Assembly session, those ten delegates introduced a bill that outlawed alcohol with the exception of its use for medicinal purposes.[22] It passed in the House by a 42-23 majority vote but, due to mass public objections, did not pass through the Senate.[23]

The establishment of the national Prohibition Party in 1869 was a transparent attempt by the prohibitionists to gain at least national recognition, if not electoral victory, for a unified cause of state and national Prohibition.[24] The Prohibition Party did bring more attention to its platform and generated some modest vote tallies at the state and national level from the late nineteenth century through the mid-1930s.[25] However, by 1896, Joshua Levering, a native of Baltimore, Maryland, was running as the Prohibition Party's presidential candidate and captured just 124,896 (0.9 percent) popular votes.[26]

During the late 1800s, due to the rising prominence of temperance crusaders, the drys became rather successful in implementing (and even enforcing) local option laws throughout the nation. Local option laws that called for the prohibition of transportation, manufacturing or sale of alcohol within a state—intrastate commerce—had even achieved moderate success in the Supreme Court ruling of *Mugler v. Kansas* (1887).[27] However, interstate commerce concerns abounded, as there were potential issues if one was transporting alcohol between wet and dry locales in different states. In *Leisy v. Hardin* (1890), the court held that the resale of alcohol is incident to importation, making imported liquor an article of interstate commerce and beyond state regulation as long as it remains in its original package.[28] Soon after the court's ruling, Congress passed the Wilson Original Package Act on August 8, 1890, which stated that "all fermented, distilled or other intoxicating liquors or liquids transported into any State or Territory or remaining therein for use, consumption, sale or storage therein, shall, upon arrival in such State or Territory be subject to the operation and effect of the laws of such State or Territory."[29] This was a setback to those teetotalers who favored the outright prohibition of alcohol. But dry organizations were maturing in organization and recruitment and were slowly but surely becoming a force to be reckoned with both politically and civically as their numbers and influence grew stronger.

Despite the modest results achieved by the Prohibition Party, it was during this period that two of the most visible prohibitionist groups in the vanguard of the political movement for both local and national prohibition were founded: the Woman's Christian Temperance Union (WCTU) in 1873 and the Anti-Saloon League (ASL) in 1893. Each of these organizations had individual state chapters and had the necessary political influence that gave the organizations a credentialed platform from which to speak and helped them raise funds and recruit members for their cause. The ASL achieved gradual legislative success in the late 1890s and the turn of the century with the proliferation of a number of local option laws throughout America, particularly in rural counties.[30] Both the ASL and WCTU were highly visible organizations in the state of Maryland during this time.

THE PASSAGE OF THE WEBB-KENYON ACT OF 1913

By the turn of the twentieth century, there was a clamor for reform of social and political institutions to achieve progress and "improve…conditions of life."[31] These reformers, or Progressives, often championed the ideal of temperance at a local level. Now, however, they had increasingly begun vocalizing their desire for alcohol *prohibition* and were seeking a federal law that would ban the manufacture, transportation and distribution of alcohol. Prohibition—at the local, state and national levels—fit into the Progressive model of social control and regulation. Historian John C. Burnham noted that "for Progressives, prohibition with its elements of moralism, social desirability, meliorism, and scientifically demonstrated need, provided a perfect vehicle for reform."[32] Perhaps no other moment or piece of legislation played a more important role in increasing the probability of a national Prohibition law than the passage of the Webb-Kenyon Act on March 1, 1913.

Richard F. Hamm, in his book *Shaping the Eighteenth Amendment*, noted that "no dry act, after the Wilson Act and before national Prohibition, was more important for the dry crusade than the Webb-Kenyon Act."[33] Before the enactment of the Webb-Kenyon Act, a resident of any state could obtain liquor directly from other states.[34] Historian Thomas Pegram explained that "most prohibition states permitted mail orders of liquor for personal consumption but strictly forbade shipments intended for retail sale."[35] The passage of the Webb-Kenyon Act would fundamentally change where, how and to whom liquor would be shipped.

The intent of the proposed bill, initially drafted by ASL member Fred S. Caldwell, was to ban the interstate transportation of liquor into areas where it would be used in violation of state law and to declare contracts for such transactions to be void.[36] Enforcement was to be left up to the states. The ASL soon found congressmen to support its bill, including Representative Morris Sheppard (D-Texas), Senator William Squire Kenyon (R-Iowa) and Representative Edwin Yates Webb (D-North Carolina). Webb and Kenyon would eventually be the main sponsors, as the Senate opted to pass the Webb bill as a substitute for the original Kenyon-Sheppard bill, which differed in the penalty phases.[37]

On February 8, 1913, the House of Representatives passed the Webb Anti-Liquor Shipment bill by an overwhelming vote of 240-65.[38] On February 10, the bill was passed by the Senate by a vote of 61-23. The bill was widely supported by both Democrats and Republicans.[39] Senator William Webb gave his first and only speech in favor of the bill by uttering this classic line: "Men, cattle, and sheep are stopped at State lines when they threaten to bring disease with them; so why not stop intoxicating liquors?"[40] The most glaring weakness of the Webb-Kenyon bill was that it provided for no federal enforcement and no penalties for breaking the law.[41] The drys, however, had always hoped that the states would enforce the act. For the drys, the simple possibility of Congress passing the act was enough of a "concurrent exercise of national and state power against liquor."[42]

Despite the constant pleas, via telegram, to oppose the bill from Baltimore liquor houses, Representative George Konig (D, Third Congressional District) of East Baltimore "was the only member of the Maryland delegation who voted against the bill, the other five lining up in its favor."[43] The other five representatives—J. Harry Covington (D, First Congressional District), J. Frederick C. Talbot (D, Second Congressional District), J. Charles Linthicum (D, Fourth Congressional District), Thomas Parran Sr. (R, Fifth Congressional District) and David J. Lewis (D, Sixth Congressional District)—were in favor of the bill. All of Maryland's representatives did, however, vote against the Davis Amendment to the bill, which would have provided harsher penalties for those breaking the law.[44] Maryland's senators, John Walter Smith (D) and William Purnell Jackson (R), voted in favor of the bill as well.

On February 10, Superintendent William H. Anderson of the Anti-Saloon League of Maryland stated that "we have whipped the liquor traffic to a standstill…after years of weary waiting and desperate fighting, we have broken through the obstructions of legislative procedure and through its various State organization, the Anti-Saloon League has focused upon Congress an absolutely irresistible demand for relief."[45] Anderson went on to praise the united temperance forces, specifically citing the WCTU for its efforts, and congratulated the ASL in Maryland for only "one of the Senators and two of the Congressmen from Maryland were supposed actually to favor the bill…from a State which is such a liquor centre."[46]

The passage of the Webb bill had stimulated a renewed fervor for statewide local option laws in Maryland. Anderson had to be happy with the ASL's success in gaining what looked to be unprecedented political support for local option. Clearly, Anderson hoped to use the momentum generated in 1913 for future ASL victories in Maryland. Ironically, however, despite the newfound political support and muscle, Superintendent Anderson was never able to achieve a statutory statewide local option bill in Maryland despite a major effort in the Maryland General Assembly in 1916—even though the ASL had been successful in earlier years in lobbying the General Assembly for various local temperance laws.[47] Despite the failure to achieve a statewide bill, the ASL could claim success in its local option efforts, for by 1917, twenty-one out of twenty-three Maryland counties had voted to go dry.

The Equitable Building, Suite 800, at 10 North Calvert Street in Baltimore, served as the headquarters for the Maryland Anti-Saloon League. *Michael T. Walsh.*

Progressives and their associated calls for reform, including temperance and local option laws, had gained a foothold in many regions of the United States, although historian James Crooks argued that Maryland "was in the mainstream but not the forefront of Progressive change."[48] Compared

William H. Anderson, superintendent of Maryland's Anti-Saloon League from 1906 to 1913. *Library of Congress, Prints and Photographs Division, Bain Collection, LC-DIG-ggbain-22393.*

to what came before, Maryland made steady and certainly effectual improvement to its social and political structure in the Progressive era, but the results, when implemented, were often limited.[49] Crooks is correct in stating that in Maryland (as was true elsewhere in the United States) Progressivism meant conservative reform, for such a statement supports the notion that Maryland, by and large, was rather conservative and traditional in its views.[50] Conceivably, Crooks's assessment may accurately provide at least some reason for why Maryland was able to favor the Webb-Kenyon Act but was unwilling to pass a statewide bill in 1916.

President William Howard Taft did veto the Webb bill, with a concurrent opinion supporting his veto by Attorney General George W. Wickersham on February 28, finding it to be unconstitutional because Congress had improperly delegated its powers over interstate commerce to the states. However, President Taft was literally days away from leaving office—he lost the 1912 presidential election to Woodrow Wilson. Therefore, on March 1, 1913, the Senate voted to override Taft's veto (63-21), and the next day the House did the same (244-95).[51] Both Maryland senators voted for the Webb bill again. Representative Konig was joined this time by Representative Parran—the reason for Parran's vote reversal was not given in historical accounts of this Congressional action—in supporting Taft's veto, but the other four representatives again supported the bill.[52]

In 1914, hoping to capitalize on the success of the Webb-Kenyon Act, there was a failed attempt at a Prohibition amendment—the Hobson-Shepard bill. It had failed simply due to too much opposition by wets in Congress.[53] However, by 1916, both the House of Representatives and the Senate were under the control of the dry faction. The drys in Congress now outnumbered the wets by a more than two-to-one margin.[54]

In Maryland, after numerous attempts by the drys in previous years, the Maryland General Assembly in 1916 passed a local option bill that would be subject to a referendum in the November election. Many of Maryland's counties, as well as Baltimore City, would finally be allowed to vote on whether to enact alcohol prohibition legislation within their boundaries. In the months leading up to the November 1916 referendum, Baltimore City had registered a majority of forty-five thousand against a local option prohibition, which for the drys was an ominous but not altogether unexpected tally.[55] As TABLE 1 indicates, when the referendum was held, Baltimore voted three to one in favor of staying wet (see the appendix for this and other tables).[56] All twenty-eight of Baltimore's wards tallied more votes against Prohibition than votes for the policy. Interestingly, the wards with the higher percentages opposed tended to have more blue-collar and immigrant populations, whereas the wards that seemed to support Prohibition tended to have more white-collar and professional populations, suggesting how sociocultural conditions may have helped in forming one's perspectives and viewpoints on Prohibition.[57]

JAMES CLARK DISTILLING COMPANY v. WESTERN MARYLAND RAIL WAYS (1917)

The constitutionality of the Webb-Kenyon Act was inevitably going to be tested in the court system. George Muller, a statistician from the United States Brewers' Association (USBA), wrote in April 1913 that even "if the Supreme Court declares the [Webb-Kenyon] act unconstitutional, it does not change the impressive fact that in the face of the united effort of all branches of the alcoholic trade, the National Congress voted for the bill."[58]

The case that came to the Supreme Court was *James Clark Distilling Company v. Western Maryland Rail Ways* (1917). The James Clark Distilling Company was located in Cumberland, Maryland, and was situated on a major commerce route—the National Pike—that had a high amount of railroad traffic. The company specialized in manufacturing and distributing the popular Braddock Maryland Rye Whiskey.[59] The company ran into problems once West Virginia passed and implemented a statewide prohibition law that no longer allowed Clark Distilling to transport alcohol through its state.[60] Western Maryland Rail Ways had refused to carry liquor into West Virginia because its point-of-sale law made shipments susceptible to seizure. With business sagging, Clark decided to fight the constitutionality of the Webb-Kenyon Act.

The Western Maryland Railways in Cumberland. The transportation company was a central participant in the Supreme Court case that upheld the constitutionality of the Webb-Kenyon Act. *Michael T. Walsh.*

Following an initial victory in U.S. District Court (1915) but then a subsequent defeat in the U.S. District Court of Appeals (1916), Clark decided to take the case to the U.S. Supreme Court.[61] Lawrence Mitchell argued for the James Clark Distilling Company that the Webb-Kenyon Act was unconstitutional because it delegated Congress's powers to the states. ASL president Wayne Wheeler and West Virginia attorney general Fred O. Blue argued that the Webb-Kenyon Act did not violate Congressional power but was, in fact, a proper regulation of commerce. They further argued that state laws fixing point-of-sales for liquor was a legitimate application of state police power.[62] On January 8, 1917, the Supreme Court, in a seven-to-two decision, upheld the Webb-Kenyon Act, declaring it constitutional and not an improper delegation of Congressional powers. Victory for the drys.

The Reed Amendment, Section 5 of the Post Office Appropriation Act (POA Act approved on March 3, 1917), took the next step toward national Prohibition. Senator James Reed (D-Missouri), who was a wet, included a dry rider into the POA Act that would ban all transportation of liquor in prohibition states (except for medicinal, sacramental and industrial purposes) because he felt that such a ban would be more than the states were willing to deal with.[63] Reed's amendment was meant to be what historian Thomas

Pegram labels a "joker," for Reed fully intended for such a measure to fail, in the process hurting the influence of what would seem to be an overreaching ASL and curtailing its shouts for national Prohibition. To Reed's dismay (in an example of unintended consequences), the bill sailed through Congress. President Wilson was troubled by the passage of this rider, but the mail had to be kept moving, especially with World War I and U.S. entry into the global war on the immediate horizon. In effect, the Reed Amendment, a "bone dry" amendment, banned all transportation and advertisement of liquor and turned the prohibition states completely dry.

On April 6, 1917, after months and years of nonintervention, the United States officially declared war on Germany. The economist Murray N. Rothbard once noted that "American entry into World War One provided the fulfillment of prohibitionists' dreams."[64] World War I proved to be a singular international event, an event wholly unrelated to American alcohol policy that garnered the necessary support for national Prohibition by both the public and the D.C. legislators. If the passage of the Webb-Kenyon Act provided the kindling for what would be the Prohibition fire, then World War I certainly can be said to have provided the needed gasoline to set off its wild flames.

The Selective Service Act, passed in May 1917, included a provision that required dry zones around all military establishments and forbade American military members from possessing or selling alcohol, even in a private residence.[65] The drys at this point were operating on two fronts and achieving remarkable success on the state and national levels after years of struggle on the national scene. In particular, the passing of the Lever Food and Fuel Control Act (and later the Wartime Prohibition Act) enabled the drys in America to use the Great War as a means to attain the goal of national Prohibition.

On July 30, 1917, the Anti-Saloon League's prohibition resolution, calling for a national Prohibition amendment to the Constitution and advocated primarily as a wartime measure, came before the U.S. Senate.[66] This resolution, with a change made to require a six-year time limit for state ratification, formed the basic foundation and language of what would ultimately be presented to the states as the Eighteenth Amendment.[67] The Senate passed the resolution on August 1, 1917, by a 65-20 vote.[68] Senator Joseph I. France (R) of Maryland voted against the resolution, while fellow Maryland senator John Walter Smith (D) was absent from the vote due to an unspecified "indisposition" (although the *New York Times* suggested that he presumably would have voted against the resolution).[69] Only a few short days later, the House of Representatives unanimously (357-0) passed the Lever Food and Fuel Control Act, and the Senate soon followed, passing the bill by a 66-7 margin (with Maryland senator Joseph France (R) once again proving to be in the minority in voting against the bill).[70] The Lever Food and Fuel Control Act effectively shut down distilleries on the grounds that the conservation and rationing of foodstuffs used in the distilling process would help the war effort.[71] This act also sharply limited the commercial production of beer.

On December 18, 1917, the House passed the ASL's prohibition resolution with three revisions to the original Senate version: (1) Congress and the states were granted concurrent power to enforce the amendment; (2) an extension of the ratification time limit was increased from six years to seven years; and (3) the date of implementation would start one year from the date of ratification of the thirty-sixth state. The House passed the bill by a 282-128 margin.[72] The majority of Maryland's representatives voted against the resolution. Representatives Charles P. Coady (D), John C. Linthicum (D), Joshua F. Talbott (D) and Sydney E. Mudd II (R) voted against the resolution, and Representatives Frederick N. Zihlman (R) and Jesse Price (D) voted in support of the resolution.[73] The Senate would subsequently concur with the joint resolution, passed by the House 47-8, which had made the change in the number of years provided for state ratification.[74] The wets were still fairly confident that thirty-six states would not ratify the amendment in the seven-year time span specified in the amendment.[75]

The *Baltimore American* published a full-page advertisement on January 23, 1918, addressed "to the People of Maryland and Members of the Maryland State Legislature," the stated purpose of which was not to debate the pros and cons of Prohibition but to express the concern about "the effect of a sweeping change in our organized law, one which should not be made without the most deliberate and mature consideration."[76] The ad contained a reasoned argument for the right of self-determination by states and by localities within the states, maintaining that the "right of the states to control local affairs has been made absolutely secure by the passage of the Webb-Kenyon and Reed Acts by Congress."[77] This was not the first time, nor the last, that the "states' rights" argument would be used in Maryland to oppose and attempt to suppress the prohibitionists' agenda.

In early February 1918, just days before Maryland was to vote on the Eighteenth Amendment, Congressman Edwin Webb (D) from North Carolina and Congressman Simeon Fess (R) from Ohio made a brief appearance at the New Theater on Lexington Street to discuss the long history of prohibition and temperance in America and why the liquor traffic must be stopped.[78] Their appearance in Baltimore can be seen as a "rallying the troops" campaign. The ratification debates in Maryland's General Assembly were just getting underway in February 1918, and the word was apparently out that Maryland, with enough of a push by the drys in the General Assembly, might soon become the sixth state to ratify the Eighteenth Amendment.

The presentation of the minority (dry) report of the Temperance Committee started the fight in the Maryland House of Delegates. The committee's report called for a postponement of ratification until the next meeting of the General Assembly in order to hold a statewide public referendum on Prohibition.[79] A letter to the editor appeared in the *Sun* on February 3 and pleaded to "let the people of Maryland decide this important matter in an orderly manner and in their own best interest, giving due and careful consideration to its influence upon their personal liberty, happiness, and general welfare."[80] When the Temperance Committee proposition was voted on, it was defeated by a 55-45 margin in the House (in favor of the drys).[81]

The debates over the national Prohibition amendment in the Maryland Senate chamber in Annapolis were heated affairs. Senator Orlando Harrison (D), a dry from Worcester County on the Eastern Shore, asked his fellow county senators if "as citizens of the counties of the State of Maryland… [we are] going to sit here and let Baltimore City drown us both with whiskey and money."[82] This comment infuriated the wets, who were surprised by the public "insinuation" that money was being used to fight and lobby against Prohibition.[83] Eventually, after an eleven-day delay, the wets were defeated. However, the resolution supporting a national Prohibition amendment was first passed by the House of Delegates due to an error in the printing of the Senate bill.[84] This error caused the state Senate to substitute the House resolution for its own.[85] On February 8, the House of Delegates—in a single day—ratified the Eighteenth Amendment.[86] On the final reading, there were fifty-eight "Yes" votes and thirty-six "No" votes.[87] The resolution passed in the Senate, eighteen votes to seven, on February 13, 1918.

The senators from Baltimore's four districts all voted against ratification. But there were more legislators in the General Assembly who hailed from already dry regions than from the more populous and wet areas like Baltimore City. In the Senate, 23 of 27 members (85 percent) were not from Baltimore, and in the House, 78 of the 102 members (76 percent) were not from Baltimore.[88] Thus, on February 13, 1918, Maryland became the sixth state in the United States to ratify the Prohibition amendment.[89] Efforts to pass a statewide prohibition bill in March 1918, however, failed by a 58-31 margin, an outcome that continued a series of dry defeats since efforts to pass Anti-Saloon League–sponsored statewide dry bills had failed three times between 1907 and 1914.[90] Several senators who supported national Prohibition believed that Maryland was obligated to go dry with the rest of the nation but were "not willing to vote it dry separately" and believed that the state had "enough dry legislation for awhile."[91]

On November 21, 1918, Congress passed the Wartime Prohibition Act, which banned the manufacture of beer and wine with an alcoholic content of more than 2.75 percent. This act was passed even though the Armistice had been signed on November 11 and a ceasefire declared by the war combatants. The Wartime Prohibition Act would go into effect on July 1, 1919, and signaled the impending death of John Barleycorn.

Finally, on January 16, 1919, Nebraska became the thirty-sixth state to ratify the Eighteenth Amendment. As stated in the amendment, national

A 1918 photo by E.T. Lewis of the storefront of Jefferson Liquor Company at 15 North Liberty Street in Baltimore. *Maryland Historical Society, SVF. Permission from the Baltimore Sun Media Group.*

Prohibition would become the law of the land one year after ratification. On January 16, 1920, the Eighteenth Amendment to the U.S. Constitution would therefore officially become the law of the land. Section I of the Eighteenth Amendment stated that "the manufacture, sale, or transportation of intoxicating liquors within, the importation thereof in, or the exportation thereof from the United States and all territory subject to the jurisdiction thereof for beverage purposes is hereby prohibited."[92] It should be noted that it was not illegal to possess or consume alcohol in *private* residences—a fact that is often forgotten.

On June 30, 1919, Baltimore's Municipal Band played "I Got the Blues" at the Recreation Pier in Fell's Point.[93] The next day, alcoholic beverages— with the exception of hard cider, which was not named on the law's list of intoxicating beverages in an oversight by those who drafted the bill— were no longer allowed to be manufactured or sold due to the Wartime Prohibition Act.[94] On July 1, 1919, the *Evening Sun* ran a political cartoon on its front page. The cartoon was entitled "Hamlet's Lament."[95] The famous

The Broadway Recreation Pier in Fell's Point was a somber venue in 1919 before Wartime Prohibition went into effect. The docks near the Pier off Thames Street were part of Spedden's Shipyard as well. *Michael T. Walsh.*

scene in which Hamlet holds the skull was parodied. Instead of Hamlet holding a skull, he is weeping and holding a jug of booze—aptly labeled as "Bill Booze"—crying out, "Alas, Alas, Poor Bill."[96] A pile of discarded bones, labeled July 1, is shown in the distance. Brewers continued the production of 2.75 percent beer because they claimed that the Wartime Prohibition Act had failed to define the alcoholic content of an "intoxicating beverage." Until the Supreme Court upheld Congress's right to define the word "intoxicating" in January 1920, 2.75 percent beer could be found on tap in Baltimore's bars.[97] Those who sold the 2.75 percent beer only needed to obtain a new liquor license from the Board of Liquor License Commissioners.[98]

Although the amendment was ratified, an enforcement measure was needed to ensure compliance with the new Prohibition law. Representative Andrew J. Volstead of Minnesota presented House of Representatives Bill No. 6810, popularly referred to as the Volstead Act, whose aim was "to prohibit intoxicating beverages and to regulate the manufacture, production, use and sale of high-proof spirits for other than beverage purposes"[99] and define that an illegal intoxicating beverage was a beverage whose alcohol content exceeded 0.5 percent by volume.[100] Title I of the act stated the following:

> The term "War Prohibition Act" used in this Act shall mean the provisions of any Act or Acts prohibiting the sale and manufacture of intoxicating liquors until the conclusion of the present war and thereafter until the termination of demobilization, the date of which shall be determined and proclaimed by the President of the United States. The words "beer, wine, or other intoxicating malt or vinous liquors" in the War Prohibition Act shall be hereafter construed to mean any such beverages which contain one-half of 1 per centum or more of alcohol by volume: Provided, That the foregoing definition shall not extend to de-alcoholized wine nor to any beverage or liquid produced by the process by which a beer, ale, porter, or wine is produced, if it contains less than one-half of 1 per centum of alcohol by volume.[101]

President Woodrow Wilson, who had just suffered a severe stroke, vetoed the Volstead Act on October 27, 1919; however, that veto was overridden by Congress.[102] Representatives William N. Andrews (R) and Frederick Zihlman (R) of Maryland voted to override Wilson's veto, while Representative Sydney Mudd II (R) voted to sustain the president's veto. Representatives John Linthicum (D), Charles Coady (D) and Carville D.

Benson (D), like many other members of the House who thought the vote would be postponed, were either not present or did not vote.[103] In the Senate, Maryland senator Joseph France (R) once more voted in the minority, opting to support the president, and Senator John Walter Smith (D) was once again absent from the chamber—as he was during the vote for the Eighteenth Amendment—during the roll call vote.[104] The Volstead Act became law on October 28, 1919.[105]

In December 1919, several newspaper editorials appeared in the *Baltimore American* that revealed and represented Baltimoreans' bitterness toward the coming implementation of the Eighteenth Amendment. A daily column that appeared regularly, "Notes and Notions," was written by a columnist with a pseudonym of "Josh Wink." Wink lamented the fact that alcohol would no longer be present for future Christmases (even though private possession and consumption of alcoholic beverages within one's own house was not illegal). His column on December 12, 1919, called "Anxious Times," expressed the wish that although the time was getting "tragically short…liquid joy will pour its short-lived wealth upon us all in time to drink a Christmas health."[106] In his December 15 column entitled "Holiday Cheer," Wink gave yet another poetic sendoff to one last public wet Christmas by encouraging his readers to "prepare for the cup Of the holiday cheer, For the flowing punch bowl, For the eggnog erst dear, For the sparkling champagne, And pledge in their flow The jovial times Soon forever to go."[107]

Prohibition Arrives

On December 15, 1919, the Supreme Court issued its opinion that the Wartime Prohibition Act was constitutional.[108] The *American* reported that "gloom fell over the wet trade" in Baltimore.[109] The paper likened the prohibitionists in Congress to "relics of the Spanish Inquisition."[110] ASL superintendent George Crabbe was pleased, noting, naïvely, that the drys didn't "believe there would ever be another saloon in the country."[111] On January 5, 1920, the Supreme Court, in a tight 5-4 vote, upheld the constitutionality of the Volstead Act.[112]

A political cartoon with possibly the most unnerving depiction of Prohibition was published on January 6, 1920, by the *Baltimore American*.[113] Titled "That's How I Got My Start," the cartoon depicted a shackled, imprisoned, grizzled man in prison garb, holding up a picture of Uncle

Sam and a barrel that reads "a bone-dry U.S."[114] His hat, sitting next to the beastly man, is labeled "Russia."[115] This cartoon clearly was meant to capture the interest of the newspaper's well-informed readers who knew that the Bolsheviks had also implemented prohibition policies in Russia.[116] It intended to equate Prohibition as the first step toward U.S. Bolshevism.

An editorial in the *Sun* on January 16, 1920, divulged the newspaper's stance on what it deemed could be the overall outcome of Prohibition: "The Prohibition Constitutional Amendment which goes into effect tonight marks a new era in American legislation and in American government. It will not necessarily be a better era or a more peaceful era. On the contrary, it is the dawn of a day, which is characterized by all the disquieting signs of a coming storm and disturbance."[117]

The editorial also criticized the prohibitionists for being "afraid to submit the question to the voters of the various States," for "if one thing in the national situation is clearer than any other, it is that this issue will not be settled till the voters of the various States have been allowed to pass upon it directly."[118]

This page and next: Captured between 1914 and 1929 (exact date unknown), this photo from Albert M. Price shows cases of Maryland's Pikesville Rye Whiskey on a beach in Bimini, a Bahamian island. Transportation of liquor between the Chesapeake region and the Bahamas kept the Coast Guard busy during the Prohibition era. *Library of Congress, Prints and Photographs Division, Albert M. Price Panoramic Photograph Collection, LC-DIG-ppss-00901.*

On January 16, the *Sun* and *Evening Sun* reported on how 530,000 gallons of liquor, valued at $12 million, would be loaded onto three Shipping Board steamships (the *Maummee, Adelheid* and *Lake Ellerslie*) and transported to the West Indies and the Bahamas Islands since the liquor could no longer be sold in Baltimore.[119] The *Lake Ellerslie* alone contained 34,667 cases of whiskey and 1,800 barrels of liquor.[120] Liquor licenses were surrendered by saloonkeepers, and liquor stores cleared the alcoholic contents off their shelves.[121] All commercial buildings/properties that had alcohol-related signage were warned that not disassembling the advertisements would warrant a first-time fine of $500.[122] Other newspaper articles described Baltimoreans stocking their cellars with cases of whiskey (which were selling at an exorbitantly high rate of $125 per case) and other assorted liquors in preparation for the long drought.[123] Such open contempt for the legislation and its supporters was evident when the president of the Anti-Prohibition League, James F. Klecks, received innumerable letters threatening bodily harm to Anti-Saloon League president J.F. Heisse, as well as musing on the possible formation of a Ku Klux Klan–like organization in Maryland

to oppose Prohibition.[124] Mr. Klecks refused to divulge the names or the letters' contents despite Heisse's request to do so. Klecks responded with the following:

> *It would be nice, wouldn't it, for me to tell the names of any of the men who wrote to me in confidence. The letters refer to him particularly. They referred to all the men who had been identified with prohibition and with that general attitude—George W. Crabbe, Dr. Howard A. Kelly, and others….If these men don't believe what I say they ought go down to the Baltimore Dry Docks and Shipbuilding Company, to Sparrow's Point and other places, where there are a lot of workmen and see what those men say about those who took away their beer.*[125]

The arrival of Prohibition on a weekend and the resulting decline of nightlife in Baltimore made the impact of Prohibition even more evident to eyewitnesses. Baltimore's first dry Saturday night was lamented by the *Evening Sun*, as it noted that "evidently, it takes more than food, lemonade, and dance music to make an evening wild."[126] Downtown Baltimore was described as being "as wild as a Baltimore county jungle and as dry as the Sahara Desert."[127] The non-alcoholic night was deemed to be a flop by the newspaper. The bouncer at one club yearned for the good old days when he used to have to throw drunks out of the establishment.[128] Now the current patrons drank iced ginger ale.[129] The *Evening Sun* reported that even the Chinese restaurants that "had sprung up like a mushroom growth" in Baltimore and offered the chop suey dish—a "favorite food to top off an evening's drinking…it acted like an anchor to keep the booze down…it was food and medicine both"—had been hurt by Prohibition.[130]

BIRTH OF A "BABY VOLSTEAD"?

In Annapolis, on February 25, 1920, wets in Maryland's General Assembly, doggedly led by William Marbury, a known wet who was active in U.S. courts attacking the constitutionality of dry laws, introduced two resolutions that aimed, albeit futilely, at voiding the Eighteenth Amendment.[131] One resolution called for a recall vote of the Maryland legislature's vote from 1918 that ratified the Eighteenth Amendment, claiming that the legislature "had no mandate from the people for its action."[132] The second resolution hoped to formulate steps that the state could take in court that would have the "so-called Eighteenth Amendment and the Volstead Act declared null and void."[133]

The wets planned a rally meeting for the Lyric Theater in Baltimore on the next Sunday to help garner support for their resolutions and their cause. The *Baltimore Sun* claimed that fourteen of twenty-seven senators favored the resolutions, but an exact count of those who favored the resolutions in the House had not been measured.[134] Later that day, as a counterpoint, ASL general counsel Wayne Wheeler addressed the General Assembly, espousing the benefits of Prohibition and the Volstead Act.[135] It was obvious to many that the Prohibition fight had really only just commenced.

Forty-seven states (out of forty-eight total at the time) passed statewide enforcement bills that came to be termed "baby Volsteads" because they essentially mimicked the language and prose of the federal Volstead Act. A "baby Volstead" sought to ensure state compliance with the national act and also put the responsibility of the enforcement of Prohibition on the state as

The Lyric Theater, shown here in 2017, served as a major venue for speeches and rallies related to Prohibition. *Michael T. Walsh.*

well as the federal governments. The exceptional state that refused to pass a "baby Volstead," despite numerous attempts to do so, was Maryland.

In March 1920, the General Assembly in Maryland began debates and drafted what were essentially two statewide prohibition enforcement bills that were completely different from each other. The bill supported by the drys was a statewide Prohibition enforcement bill that was publicly referred to as the McBride bill, named after its sponsor, delegate Edgar McBride (R) of Frederick, Maryland. This bill, promoted by the Maryland Anti-Saloon League, was a "baby Volstead" act that prohibited the sale of beverages containing more than 0.5 percent alcohol by volume.

Before the wets in the House of Delegates countered with a statewide bill, two Maryland Senate members attempted to gain the attention and potential action of Congress. On March 8, Senators J. Frank Parran (R) of Calvert County and Oliver S. Metzerott (R) of Prince George's County introduced a joint resolution "memorializing Congress to amend the Volstead Act so that beverages containing 3.5 percent alcohol may be manufactured and sold."[136] The *Baltimore Sun* reported that Senator Metzerott was a known prohibitionist who still advocated the need for national Prohibition; however, Metzerott felt the Volstead Act was too drastic and that 3.5 percent beverages were, as the *Sun* termed, "not ordinarily intoxicating."[137] Parran and Metzerott were both from counties that were generally recognized as dry. Yet the *Sun* reported that there was seemingly a "great change in sentiment" in some of Maryland's dry counties, indicating that public opinion toward the Eighteenth Amendment in certain dry regions in Maryland may have already begun to transform just a few short months after implementation![138] The joint resolution, however, never passed.

In the days following the announcement of the joint resolution, delegate Willis Jones (D) from Baltimore City's Third District became the lead sponsor on House Bill No. 554 in Maryland's House of Delegates that would legalize the sale of alcoholic liquors (beer, light wine and cider) in the 1–3.5 percent range in Maryland.[139] On March 17, Governor Albert C. Ritchie endorsed the Jones bill, stating that it would "constitute a protest by the people of Maryland against the denial of their right to express their wishes upon this important question, and will be an indication of their desire that the Volstead act be amended."[140] Most importantly, the Jones bill was drafted and written with a keen eye toward the upcoming decision that would be delivered by the Supreme Court on the National Prohibition Cases. If the Volstead Act itself was declared unconstitutional, then the Jones bill would become the state enforcement act "till there is concurrent legislation as-provided in the Eighteenth Amendment." If the Supreme Court decided that states could pass such legislation or if the Volstead Act was declared unconstitutional, Marylanders would be allowed to "make wine and cider for their own use and make and sell beverages containing alcohol not to exceed three and one-half percent of alcohol by volume."[141]

On March 19, the House of Delegates, by a 62-39 vote, rejected the McBride bill but passed the Jones bill on for a third reading. The *Sun* noted that the balance of power in the legislature had begun to lean toward the wets.[142] With the defeat of the McBride bill, it was even argued by Speaker Millard E. Tydings (D) of Havre de Grace that unless the Jones bill was passed, there would be no state enforcement act at all if the Volstead Act was declared unconstitutional by the upcoming Supreme Court decision.[143] However, the General Assembly session came to a close in April 1920, and as the *Sun* reported, "the result was that nothing was done" on the liquor question.[144]

The Jones bill never reached a definitive roll call vote in the House. Why? A headline from the *Sun*—"Teeth Drawn from State Wet Measure"— might partially explain why the Jones bill never reached maturation.[145] Despite Governor Ritchie's strong backing of the bill, there were enough detractors of the bill in the legislature to force the original drafted bill to undergo significant revisions. In particular, delegate Stephen Gambrill (D) of Howard County attacked the Jones bill and was successful in ensuring that it would be open to amendments on its third reading. The amendments, which were approved (likely reluctantly) by Governor Ritchie, provided that the bill would not go into effect unless the Supreme Court decided that "such legislation is within the power of the States to enact or unless the Supreme Court declares the Volstead Prohibition Enforcement Act unconstitutional."[146] Changing the bill to include this provision effectively made the passage of the bill a moot point for the bill's usefulness, as it was now exclusively tied to the outcome and decision of the Supreme Court.

The Supreme Court rendered its decision on the National Prohibition Cases (253 U.S. 350 [1920]) on June 7, 1920. In a unanimous 9-0 decision, the court ruled to uphold the validity of the Eighteenth Amendment and ruled that the Volstead Act was constitutional.[147] Effectively, the court ruled that states could "independently implement an equivalent or more strict Prohibition but could not relax the terms of the law within their borders."[148] The court also noted that "because the Eighteenth Amendment granted the states concurrent power of enforcement, it also required states to adhere to the federal definition of intoxicating beverage. However, the amendment did not require states to take any particular enforcement action."[149]

The court's decision ensured that legislation like the Jones bill could not be passed in Maryland. However, the court's ruling also made certain that Maryland was not required to take any enforcement action. The drys in Maryland were not confident enough to have a statewide referendum on the issue that would be determined by the voting citizens.[150] The risk was too high, for there was a real possibility of public denouncement of the "baby Volstead" act that would be too embarrassing and could have seriously hindered federal enforcement, which was already tenuously arranged.

Chapter 3

SOCIOCULTURAL IMPACTS
OF PROHIBITION

SPIRITS AND THE SPIRITUAL:
PROHIBITION MIXES WITH RELIGION

Maryland, which was founded as a religiously tolerant state, remained one of the more liberal states with respect to religious beliefs in the twentieth century.[151] TABLE 2 illustrates the robust congregation numbers of many of Baltimore's denominations.[152] Yet Maryland provided a highly volatile battleground with respect to religion and Prohibition, particularly in the juxtaposing differing views of the policy between Protestants and Catholics in Baltimore.

Henry S. Dulaney, treasurer of the Anti-Saloon League of Maryland and co-founder of the Baltimore-based Resinol Chemical Company—the company that produced Resinol, a medicated ointment for skin irritations—wrote in the *Manufacturer's Record* that Christians should advocate Prohibition for the betterment of mankind's morals as well as their own purity of the soul. Dulaney believed that Prohibition would benefit "the laboring man" economically, physically and spiritually.[153] "As a Christian man," he wrote, "I feel it is my duty, in every way that I possibly can, to advance the cause of Prohibition in this and every other country of the world."[154]

In contrast, Samuel C. Appleby, the executive secretary of the Maryland Anti-Prohibition League, published a short work in 1920 called *Positive Proof that the Bible Is Against Prohibition*.[155] Appleby concluded that the Bible preached moderation but not prohibition. He wrote that what he "did find however was that the use of wine is commended and its abuse everywhere discouraged. There is not one word favorable to Prohibition; but, on the contrary, Prohibition is clearly and definitely condemned by the scriptures."[156] Appleby also examined the Last Supper story as told in the Gospel of Matthew, in which Jesus drinks wine transubstantiated into his blood. Appleby noted that many Christian prohibitionist leaders had called wine a poison, even though Jesus called it his blood.[157] Because the Volstead Act outlawed wine, Appleby accused the Anti-Saloon League of thinking that it knew what was better for people than Jesus Christ himself.[158]

Nationally, and in Maryland as well, the Christian denominations most commonly supporting Prohibition were within the Methodist, Presbyterian, Baptist and Congregationalist churches.[159] These Protestant denominations were active in organizations like the WCTU and the Anti-Saloon League, whose members were composed primarily of middle-class, devout religious people who felt that alcohol was badly damaging American morals and health.[160]

Baltimore was the location of the annual meeting of the Presbyterian General Assembly—the governing body of the Presbyterian Church in the United States—at the Lyric Theater in May 1926.[161] At this meeting, Senator William Borah (R) of Idaho addressed the assembly and attacked the idea and calls for a national referendum on the Eighteenth Amendment. The willingness and desire to perform such a speech in predominantly wet Baltimore reveals the confidence, and indeed moral righteousness, of dry leaders during the era. Certainly, little fear existed between wets and drys in public or private debate. Theirs was an open forum battle in which both sides hoped to attract attention and support. In 1930, the Presbyterian Church attracted the attention of Maryland's wet Senator Millard E. Tydings. Tydings delivered a speech on the Senate floor that incorporated a survey conducted by Reverend Dr. J.W. Claudy—the general director of the Department of Moral Welfare of the Presbyterian Board of Christian Education—about drinking habits of high school pupils and their attitudes toward Prohibition. The results—25 percent of high school boys and girls drank intoxicating liquor, 33 percent of the high school students polled answered that they received no instruction about the use of alcohol and about 30 percent answered that Prohibition was not beneficial to the nation—prompted Tydings to remark that "coming from that source, at least, the drys will not question its authenticity."[162]

Baptist support of Prohibition was common as well. Joshua Levering was a presidential nominee of the national Prohibition Party in 1896 and

Harris and Ewing's 1935 photograph of Havre de Grace, Maryland native Senator Millard Tydings (D) of Maryland. *Library of Congress, Prints and Photographs Division, Harris and Ewing Collection, LC-DIG-hec-39655.*

was a member at Eutaw Place Baptist Church in Baltimore.[163] Levering also served as the vice-president of the Southern Baptist Convention, was the commissioner of the Maryland Baptists Union Association and was a charter member of the University Baptist Church in North Baltimore.[164] In another example of Baptist support, one African American Baptist pastor, Reverend J. Timothy Boddie of the Union Baptist Church in Baltimore, expressed great pessimism about the return of beer in April 1933:

> *It appears that the government is more concerned about the revenue obtained through the sale of beer than it is about the moral, social, and religious integrity of its citizens....Prohibition presented any number of unsolved problems but these problems are minute in comparison to those that will arise with the return of beer. It will be a jump from an unsolved cross-word puzzle to an unfathomed jig-saw puzzle.[165]*

Thus, as late as April 1933, at least one community leader in Baltimore supported Prohibition and felt that its continuance was good for his congregation and others as well.

METHODISTS IN MARYLAND

In Baltimore and Maryland, Methodism was one of the largest and most important religious organizations. In 1784, Baltimore became "the cradle of Methodism in America" when the Methodist Episcopal Church was officially formed at the Lovely Lane Meeting House in Baltimore City.[166] Methodists in Baltimore and Maryland generally favored Prohibition. In fact, Reverend Edward L. Wilson of Baltimore's Madison Avenue Methodist Episcopal Church attested that for Methodists, Maryland was the cradle of the dry movement, alluding to both the Washingtonians who began in Baltimore in the 1840s and the founding of the Methodist Episcopal Church in Baltimore.[167] With an already potent delegation on the Eastern Shore, Methodist Prohibitionists targeted Baltimore, home to hundreds of churches and hundreds of thousands of people, in the hopes of gaining some much-needed supporters of Prohibition in the wet city. For example, on December 12, 1919, the *Baltimore American* reported that Wayne B. Wheeler, the national counsel for the Anti-Saloon League, held a meeting at Mount Vernon Place Methodist Episcopal Church and implored all churches to assist in enforcing Prohibition laws once they became official.[168]

Wayne Bidwell Wheeler, general counsel and president of the national Anti-Saloon League. Photo taken on January 5, 1920, by Harris and Ewing, just fifteen days prior to Prohibition taking effect. *Library of Congress, Prints and Photographs Division, LC-DIG-ds-00046.*

One of the most well-known national Prohibitionists was Bishop James Cannon Jr. of the Methodist Episcopal Church, South. Although Cannon made his name as a Prohibitionist from Virginia, he was born and raised in Salisbury on Maryland's notoriously dry Eastern Shore, where his

Harris and Ewing's 1932 photograph of Bishop James Cannon during a Prohibition women's rally at the Capitol in Washington, D.C. *Library of Congress, Prints and Photographs Division, Harris and Ewing Collection, LC-DIG-hec-36796.*

attendance at Asbury Church influenced his ideas about temperance.[169] As the Prohibition era progressed, Cannon's once sublime reputation became tarnished due to accusations and allegations of adultery and gambling.[170] Cannon's fall from grace during the 1920s mirrored that of another well-known Methodist prohibitionist, William H. Anderson (superintendent of Maryland's Anti-Saloon League from 1906 to 1913), who was convicted of forging ASL financial records in 1924. Improprieties by men like Cannon and Anderson provided wets with anti-Prohibition propaganda, allowing for Prohibitionists to be criticized as hypocrites for championing moral ideals that they themselves, so enticed by vice, could not live up to.[171]

On January 18, 1920, many local churches celebrated the beginning of Prohibition by observing "Dry Sunday," as the first dry Sunday in U.S. history.[172] One of the main celebrations took place at the Union Square Methodist Episcopal Church on Lombard and Calhoun Streets, whose pastor, Reverend Dr. J. Fred Heisse, was president of Maryland's Anti-Saloon League.[173] A special request by the governing body of the national Methodist Episcopal Church told local Methodist Episcopal churches to observe the day as "Prohibition Sunday."[174] On January 25, Reverend Heisse and the Anti-Saloon League held a rally at the Lyric Theater to discuss the "ways and means of enforcing national Prohibition."[175] This was the first public meeting in Maryland given to analyzing how Prohibition would be enforced.[176]

The *Baltimore Southern Methodist* was the official newspaper of the Baltimore Conference of the Methodist Episcopal Church, South (MECS), which had about 2,500 registered members in its Baltimore congregation in 1916. The Baltimore Conference encompassed a large region that expanded beyond the city and state borders into neighboring regions in West Virginia and Washington, D.C. The newspaper was quite vocal in its support for Prohibition and expressed the opinion, presumably still shared by many Methodists in Baltimore and elsewhere in 1932, that the idea of calling on state conventions to act on repeal was a mistake.[177] On September 12, 1933, the day that voting was held to determine Maryland's delegates to the Constitutional Convention, Methodist women on the Eastern Shore stayed true to their temperance cause. In Easton, women from the Ebenezer Old Side Methodist Episcopal Church shouted at passersby to vote for the "retention of the Prohibition amendment."[178] They then returned to the inside of the church to pray until the poll results were returned.[179] Suffice to say, their prayers were not answered on that day, as the election results all but ensured that Maryland would repeal the Eighteenth Amendment.

PROTESTANT OPPOSITION TO PROHIBITION

Despite the overwhelming support given to Prohibition by Protestants in Baltimore and Maryland, there were some denominations that did not always fervently support Prohibition. The thirty-fourth international Lutheran Walther League convention was held in Baltimore in July 1926 and was attended by nearly five thousand delegates of the church. Theodore Graeber of Concordia Seminary in St. Louis noted that "National Prohibition by force, blue laws, anti-tobacco law and other reform legislation are hostile to the best interest of the State and religion."[180] Graeber added that keeping the separation of church and state was of vital importance and that such moral legislation blurred those lines of separation. Baltimore native and Presbyterian theologian J. Gresham Machen openly opposed Prohibition and disagreed with the Presbyterian Church's support of the policy, feeling that the issue was of a political and not a spiritual nature. The issue, among many others, contributed to Machen breaking off from the church and forming the Orthodox Presbyterian Church.[181]

By 1926, even some pastors of Protestant denominations who once favored Prohibition at its onset had changed their minds. Episcopalian Reverend Dr. H.P. Almon Abbot, rector of Grace and St. Peter's Church on Baltimore's Park Avenue, and Dr. William Page Dame, of Memorial Church in Bolton Hill, publicly announced that they would campaign for temperance and not Prohibition. They felt that they should do what the Bible teaches, and they believed that the Bible teaches temperance, not Prohibition.[182]

Two other dissenting voices in Baltimore that arose were those of the African Methodist Episcopal Church (AME) and the African Methodist Episcopal Zion Church (AME Zion). In 1933, Reverend G.M. Edwards, pastor of the Pennsylvania Avenue AME Zion Church, offered his own opinion on Prohibition in the *Afro-American*, just days before beer was about to make its return to the city:

> *Prohibition has always been a fake and one of the biggest pieces of hypocrisy from my point of view....Since Prohibition we did not know what home had or did not have beer; now we will have the saloon and everyone will know. I am not a party to it, crawling, walking, or flying, but it is hard to tell a man what he should not have when you have it on the shelf ready to sell to him....Beer and liquor are not the greatest evils in the world, neither are they the main roots.[183]*

Although some leaders of the AME Church in Maryland had originally worked hand in hand with the Maryland Anti-Saloon League between 1908 and 1915, the experiences under Prohibition from 1920 to 1933 must have altered the opinions of some of its leaders. By April 1933, the AME Church believed that the repeal of Prohibition would be helpful to society.[184] Two AME reverends, Reverend King and Reverend Rice, were not as vocal about the prospects of repeal as Reverend Edwards of AME Zion but nevertheless indicated that the return of beer, wine and liquor might be helpful in curtailing the economic effects of the Depression. Reverend King questioned if beer's return would really help the stagnant U.S. economy (hoping that it would).[185] Reverend Rice echoed King's thoughts and also stated that he believed that the principles of Prohibition were reasonable, but that legislating religion and morals was not possible.[186]

In one volatile (and, by today's standards, quite bigoted) example of Protestant opposition to Prohibition, Reverend W.A. Crawford-Frost of St. Mary's Episcopal Church in Emmorton, Maryland, framed the Prohibition question as a battle between two competing religions—Christianity and Islam. He asked whether Americans should follow Jesus or Muhammad regarding the liquor question. Crawford-Frost described that Jesus's first public act was to change water to wine at the wedding at Cana. In contrast, he stated that Muhammad warned that liquor was a "curse to humanity."[187] The reverend asked:

> *What does history show as the answer to this question? The followers of Mahomet [sic] have always been inefficient, dishonest, and cruel, and are so at this present moment....The Christian nations, which are the greatest users of alcoholic beverages, are the most kindly and humane in care of the sick, the orphans, the aged and the homeless. They are the most efficient and the most honest.*[188]

Crawford-Frost received numerous criticisms of his incendiary sermon, yet he replied with another impassioned sermon. He stressed his ultimate belief that Jesus's actions regarding alcohol were "right" and Muhammad's sermons were "wrong." Crawford-Frost then described that Muhammad's sword, "a sword of conversion," was now being wielded by the U.S. federal government.[189]

ROMAN CATHOLICISM

The principal Christian denomination opposing Prohibition, nationally and in Maryland, was the Roman Catholic Church. Maryland was named for Catholic Queen Consort Henrietta Maria (wife of King Charles I of England) by the Catholic Calvert family after they landed in Southern Maryland at St. Mary's City in 1632.[190] The Calverts founded Maryland as a Catholic territory, as a land that would be free of the persecution of Catholics. Baltimore itself was the oldest Catholic diocese in the United States and was the only archdiocese in the nation until 1846.[191] In 1916, Roman Catholics in Baltimore, many of whom had newly immigrated to America, made up 46 percent of Baltimore's total denominations membership.[192]

With respect to alcohol, the Catholics, like many Lutherans and Episcopalians, were typically moderate in their attitudes.[193] The use of sacramental wine was, of course, integral to Catholic services (transubstantiation, or the belief that the sacramental wine is transformed into the blood of Jesus Christ, is a central belief for Catholics). In 1920, the Roman Catholic Church did receive a special reprieve from the Volstead Act, for the church was allowed to use wine for Communion. Reverend E.J. Connelly, the chancellor of the Archdiocese of Baltimore, was in charge of making sure that all Maryland Roman Catholic parishes received sacramental wine.[194] Roman Catholic parishioners also tended to enjoy alcohol as part of their daily lives. Parish communities, especially in Baltimore, often ethnic in makeup (Germans, Italians, Poles and so on), typically celebrated old-country traditions such as drinking, and not surprisingly, parishioners frequented saloons. Some, like many German Catholics, worked in the alcohol industry, particularly Baltimore's breweries, which were often quintessentially German in name and in the style of beer produced.

The most important person presenting the general Roman Catholic views on Prohibition in Baltimore and Maryland was James Cardinal Gibbons, who served Maryland from 1877 until his death in 1921. The cardinal did not support Prohibition for several reasons. First, Cardinal Gibbons felt that Prohibition infringed on personal liberty and individual rights, which were at the core of Christian teachings and American liberty.[195] He also believed that much stronger and more potent alcohol-based drugs were available over the counter at the local pharmacy (although these drugs were intended for medicinal purposes) and should have been banned before alcohol.[196] The third reason that Gibbons gave was that he thought that the dry forces and legislators behind the Prohibition amendment were undemocratic because their personal agendas were not wholly representative of public opinion.[197] Finally, Cardinal Gibbons believed that Prohibition would only spawn an increased bootleg trade in alcohol, for people would react with hostility to having their personal liberty invaded by government.[198]

In 1916, Cardinal Gibbons denounced the statewide prohibition bill that was being considered in the General Assembly, stating that it would be "impossible" to enforce, especially in a city the size of Baltimore, that such a law would "interfere with personal liberty and rights and create hypocrisy in the people…[and that] it would deprive the State of a large revenue without accomplishing results and that too, at a time when both the city and state are very much in need of the revenue produced."[199] Gibbons said that he strongly favored temperance and moderation and that local option was a sound, democratic principle.

Cardinal Gibbons also feuded with ASL superintendent William Anderson in a war of words, as Anderson accused the cardinal of trying to cause sectarian dispute by blaming prohibition on the Protestants with "incendiary utterances" and opposing prohibition because many of the proprietors of Maryland's distilleries and saloons just so happened to be members of his church.[200] Cardinal Gibbons, however, was at heart a peaceful man and openly tolerant of other religious denominations, as evidenced by his sanctioning of a Billy Sunday (the eminent evangelist and prohibitionist) campaign in Baltimore in 1915.[201] Even other Protestants and prohibitionists recognized that Gibbons respected the views of people of all faiths. For example, in a letter to the editor of the *Sun*, a Branchville, Maryland resident, who was a Presbyterian and a prohibitionist, scolded those who had written letters to the *Sun* questioning the cardinal's "integrity and sincerity for opposing the Prohibition amendment to the Constitution."[202] The letter, which praised Gibbons for profoundly affecting the writer's spiritual life, provides an example in which people from religious denominations could disagree and still provide respect for one another.

Although the majority of Roman Catholics opposed Prohibition, some did support the Eighteenth Amendment. An interesting juxtaposition to Cardinal Gibbons's views on Prohibition was those given by Monsignor Foley of Baltimore. Monsignor Foley, a self-proclaimed prohibitionist who was born and raised in Baltimore, was the pastor of St. Paul's Catholic Church in Baltimore.[203] In 1930, Foley stated that Prohibition was a moral and political question and that law "can make many men conclude that

Right: A 2017 photograph of the Basilica of the National Shrine of the Assumption of the Blessed Virgin Mary, built by Benjamin Latrobe, and the Cardinal Gibbons Statue sculpted by Harold Schaller and Betti Richard, located at 409 Cathedral Street in Baltimore. *Michael T. Walsh.*

Below: James Cardinal Gibbons, seen here in full regalia in 1920, one year before his death. Gibbons was one of Baltimore's and the nation's most outspoken opponents of Prohibition. *Library of Congress, Prints and Photographs Division, Bain Collection, LC-DIG-npcc-02369.*

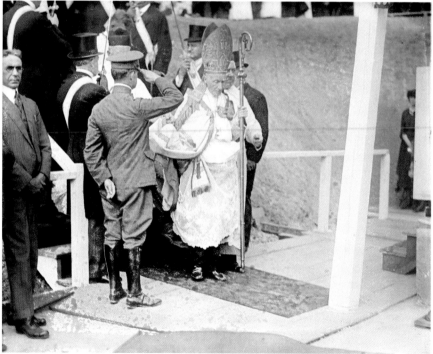

order and decency and cleanliness and some other virtues are at least mighty good things to observe."[204] Foley also recited the familiar fear that the wets of 1930 would bring back the old saloon with its violence and corruption.[205]

Foley's opinion on Prohibition evidently differed from the opinion of most Roman Catholics, certainly of the many who were parishioners at his downtown Baltimore church. But the monsignor's statement is important because it reveals that not all Roman Catholics opposed Prohibition. The diversity and religious tolerance of many Marylanders allowed for these religions to express varying degrees of opinion on Prohibition.

MARYLAND WOMEN AND PROHIBITION

In 1921, Reverend Dr. J.F. Heisse recognized the fact that enforcing Prohibition in Maryland had thus far been problematic. But he emphasized the idea of hope, particularly due to one key new voting segment of the population: women, who had gained the right of suffrage with the passage of the Nineteenth Amendment in 1920. Heisse explained that "there will be a Legislature elected in Maryland this year that will sustain the Federal law. The women are in control now and we will get the law that we could not get last time. The women will clean up things."[206] It should be duly noted that in Maryland, Governor Ritchie and other political leaders opposed the Nineteenth Amendment on the same grounds that many of them opposed the Eighteenth Amendment—they felt that the issue of women's suffrage should be decided by each individual state, not by the federal government.[207] Opponents argued that the individual state should have the right to determine its own laws for women's suffrage (as they also should for alcohol prohibition). The State of Maryland did not ratify the Nineteenth Amendment until 1941, more than twenty years after the amendment became constitutional law.

The Woman's Christian Temperance Union (WCTU) was one of the pioneers of the Prohibition movement and spearheaded the effort to gain statewide dry laws as well as a national Prohibition. As early as 1914, there were more than four thousand regular members of the WCTU and countless supporters, both women and men.[208] The WCTU had local chapters in the state that were strengthened by their ties to the Maryland Anti-Saloon League. Most of these women came from an upper-middle-class background and were vocal in their insistence on Progressive reform.[209]

A delegation of Maryland women at the U.S. Capitol for the 1926 Prohibition hearings. *Library of Congress, Prints and Photographs Division, National Photo Company Collection, LC-DIG-npcc-15712.*

A prime example of a Maryland woman who was supportive of Prohibition was Catherine Rebecca Greene. Greene, who lived in Carroll County, made various entries in her notebook from 1916 to 1918 that reveal some activities of the Sandyville Loyal Temperance Legion (SLTL), an organization in which she was an active participant. Her notebooks, now housed in the Historical Society of Carroll County, contained "yells" and cheers, such as the example here, which expressed the organization's feelings about Prohibition in Maryland:

> *Pro, hi, bi, ti, on tie on to Prohibition.*
> *I can't vote, neither can Ma.*
> *If the County goes wet,*
> *blame it on Pa.*

Who are we,
can you tell?
We are the Sandyville L. T.L.

Are we in it?
Yes we are.
Sandyville Legioners,
Rah, Rah, Rah.

Saloons must go.
Maryland, Maryland,
She says so.

Prohibition once,
Prohibition twice
Statewide Prohibition
Isn't that nice?

1917 My! My! My!
1918 Dry! Dry! Dry!
You all want her dry
That's the reason why.

Beer and whisky,
They're a curse.
We drink water,
Safety first.[210]

One indicator of women's support of Prohibition and its enforcement in the early 1920s is the results of the *Literary Digest*'s public opinion poll on Prohibition in 1922. The *Digest* conducted an unscientific straw poll (with people randomly selected from state voters' lists) that aimed to measure Americans' opinions and preferences regarding Prohibition. The total poll returns included the main poll, the women's poll and also a separate factory workers' poll (in which all workers were males). These polls have been criticized by some historians as exaggerating wet sentiment. They are clearly unscientific public opinion polls, but they are really one of the only existing measures that historians have to gauge public opinion toward the Prohibition policy, including the remarkable statistics of the women's vote in 1922.[211]

As part of this poll, the *Literary Digest* conducted a randomly drawn special women's sample, effectively asking 2.2 million women if they were for enforcement, modification or repeal. Once polling was complete in September 1922, there was a total ballot return of 922,383, of which 108,847 ballots (12 percent of total returns) were for the special women's poll. This was a very small number since 2.2 million ballots had been sent out to American women. The *Digest* duly noted that it was surprised, especially in comparison to the men (who accounted for 813,536, or 88 percent, of the returned ballots), by how few ballots were returned by women.[212] TABLES 3 and 4 show the national poll results, and TABLE 5 reveals the poll results returned by Marylanders.[213] Significantly, Maryland was the *only* state that had more votes for repeal than for present enforcement and/or modification.

If the vote tabulations in the *Digest* poll are an indication, women in the state of Maryland were definitely more conflicted about the issue of Prohibition compared to the overall national women's poll. The final ballots that were received by the *Literary Digest* from Maryland women indicated that although Maryland women still preferred present enforcement or modification over outright repeal, the results in Maryland were much closer than the results in the national poll. Examining the total national poll indicated that an overwhelming number of women polled—81.2 percent—favored Prohibition in some form. This finding suggests that although Maryland women may have still been more likely to be dry or desire modification or present enforcement (68.2 percent), they were much more likely to be wet than their counterparts in other states. In fact, the *Literary Digest* poll tabulated Maryland's women as the third wettest in the nation, behind only New York and New Jersey.[214]

On the night before Prohibition began in 1920, women in the Baltimore chapter of the WCTU gathered at their headquarters to celebrate and revel in the "bright years ahead."[215] However, once Prohibition came to Maryland, even the many women who favored Prohibition became frustrated because of the lack of enforcement in the state. An all-day conference held by the WCTU in May 1922 at the Ebenezer Methodist Episcopal Church in Easton on the Eastern Shore tackled the issue of enforcement and how women might combat violators of the Volstead Act.[216] In October 1924, the *Baltimore Sun* reported on another WCTU convention in which Mary Haslup, president of Maryland's chapter of the WCTU, gave a derisive speech about Maryland's lawlessness.[217] Haslup criticized Maryland for being disloyal to federal law by refusing to pass a state enforcement act. Haslup stated that Maryland could never match the loyalty displayed by a state such as Kansas. Even in 1924,

Haslup still ardently felt that despite its setbacks in enforcement, Prohibition was a worthy policy for America and Maryland would eventually obey and effectively comply with the Prohibition laws. Haslup's belief in Maryland's compliance proved to be incorrect.

By 1932, the WCTU was experiencing more frustration as the prospect of repeal became more likely. Haslup expressed "great sorrow" when the national Democratic Party's plank favored repeal, calling the stance "a mistake."[218] Even though she was a registered Democrat, she felt that the Democrats had abandoned the cause, and she vowed to support only those who shared her principles.[219] In September 1932, the Baltimore unit of the WCTU convened its annual convention, denounced FDR's presidential candidacy and announced that the Union would "vote only for stand pat drys in the November elections."[220] Unfortunately for the group, there were no major presidential candidates in 1932 who shared in its stated cause.

Women's attitudes toward Prohibition began to change through the decade of the 1920s. On their eighty-seventh birthdays in 1927, twin sisters Susan Perkins and Louisa Sherlock of Maryland—who proclaimed to be direct descendants of legendary frontiersman Daniel Boone—revealed the changing notions in American society, especially regarding women. The sisters declared that Prohibition was "a farce," for the law was simply not being effectively enforced. The sisters reminisced and talked about the parties they once had where they could have toddy and some eggnog legally, without consequence.[221] The twins then stated that they were very much different than the modern flappers, who they deemed should trade in their lipstick and rouge and do more housework. While such a statement seems to suggest that these elderly women were perturbed by the way they felt "liberated" women in the 1920s acted and behaved, the sisters seemed to indicate that Prohibition was partly to blame for what they deemed to be inappropriate social behavior and suspect moral aptitude.

By 1932, women in Maryland were playing an active role in the effort to repeal Prohibition by joining the Women's Organization for National Prohibition Reform (WONPR). In 1929, Pauline Sabine, a former supporter of Prohibition, founded the organization, and its membership rose steadily, reaching about 1.5 million members by 1933.[222] WONPR's platform stated that Prohibition had fostered a "criminal class," set off a crime wave and "threatened their homes and the welfare of their children."[223] In addition, WONPR also believed that national Prohibition was fundamentally wrong because it conflicted "with the basic American principle of local home rule and destroys the balance established by the framers of our government, between powers delegated to the federal authority and those reserved to the sovereign state or to the people themselves."[224]

In order to gain members, WONPR advertised a mass meeting at Baltimore's Ford's Theater for March 19, 1932, by having a steam calliope playing and handbills distributed in downtown Baltimore.[225] In May 1932, the Baltimore chapter of WONPR began a campaign in which it set out to get the signatures of women who opposed Prohibition.[226] The goal was to have thirty thousand members in the organization, and they gained one thousand new members on the first day.[227] WONPR was fairly successful in its campaign, for it attracted men to its organization as well as women, even though men were prohibited from being members. The men, whose attentions were drawn to the anti-Prohibition propaganda banners hanging from WONPR headquarters, were directed to join Edgar Allan Poe Jr.'s Maryland Battalion of the Crusaders, which was a similar organization.[228] In December 1932, the *Evening Sun* reported that WONPR's new goal was to have fifty thousand members—it had fifteen thousand members—and to assemble local units in the remaining thirteen counties in Maryland that had not yet joined.[229]

A Baltimore contingent of the WONPR also attended the national meeting in New Jersey and voted for a resolution to approve any beer bill that would appear before Congress.[230] Thus, when beer returned to Baltimore, the WONPR gave it its full blessing. When the repeal of Prohibition became a reality, Governor Ritchie thanked the women of Maryland who joined the repeal effort and helped the wets on to victory.[231]

German Americans

Out of all the immigrant groups that arrived and settled in Baltimore in the mid- to late nineteenth and early twentieth centuries, the Germans had the largest presence in the city. Baltimore had established a successful maritime trade with Bremen in the nineteenth century, and this trading route led many Germans to settle in Baltimore and Maryland.[232] There were about thirty-four thousand German Americans (combined native-born and second-generation) in Baltimore alone in 1900.[233] By 1914, that number had increased to ninety-four thousand (12.8 percent using the 1920 census).[234]

German Americans became actively involved in questions regarding the prohibition of alcoholic beverages in Baltimore. An early example shows that in the late 1800s, the German Americans in Baltimore formed the Baltimore chapter of the Independent Citizens' Union. This union advocated political reforms to create a clean and graft-free government.[235] The union also fought the blue laws, which forbade public entertainment on Sundays.[236] The union eventually joined the National German-American Alliance in 1899, which became "the largest organization of a racial, national group in American history."[237] According to Dieter Cunz, the alliance focused its efforts on opposing alcohol prohibition, which provided "the common platform upon which all of them could unite."[238]

German Americans openly opposed prohibitionists in the early 1900s. The *Baltimore Correspondent*, a weekly German American newspaper, provided many of Baltimore's German Americans' pointed opinions on the issue of Prohibition.[239] Many of these citizens (about a quarter of whom were also Catholic) viewed the consumption of alcohol as part of their customs and heritage from the old country. German Americans believed that prohibitionists attacked an integral element of their ethnic culture.

By the mid-1910s, World War I and anti-German sentiment had enabled prohibitionists to persuade most congressmen that Prohibition would be a sign of American patriotism. Anti-German sentiment arose in many parts of the United States, and in Baltimore and Maryland as well, as the loyalty of German Americans was questioned.[240] Many of Baltimore's German Americans tried to become more "Americanized" and thus became less vocal in their opposition to Prohibition.[241] The push for Prohibition occurring while America was fighting a war against Germany provided a perfect storm for drys, who could now effectively silence German American brewers' arguments that beer should not be subjected to any dry laws. The drys simply had to reinforce and project the German American as the possible enemy or hostile to the American public.

Baltimore's large German American population suffered as a result of Prohibition. The German breweries were a major reason why Baltimore was an important brewing town. With the enactment of Prohibition, German Americans lost many jobs in the brewery plants. Also noteworthy is that the loss of the breweries contributed to the potential loss of the German American cultural traditions of (legally) drinking beer.[242]

By the time beer made its return to Baltimore in April 1933, resentment against German Americans had ebbed substantially since the end of World War I (and still several years before renewed hostilities with Germany due to the commencement of World War II). Indeed, the return of beer featured the "Germanic touch of schmaltz and nostalgia" and German beer gardens.[243] Many of the post-Prohibition breweries, much like their predecessors, had German American owners as well as brewers and staff. The German American heritage was once again celebrated in Baltimore and Maryland and elsewhere in the United States. But the costs of Prohibition to the German American community could never really be wholly redeemed. Prohibition had taken its toll.

H.L. MENCKEN: BALTIMORE'S MOST PROMINENT GERMAN AMERICAN

H.L. Mencken, the "Sage of Baltimore" and one of the city's most prolific citizens and ambassadors, wrote for the *Sun* papers, as well as for the *American Mercury*.[244] Mencken, a German American, was a staunch "wet." He even coined a term—*ombibulous*—to describe his prejudice in favor of alcohol and against the restriction of personal freedom that Prohibition imposed on the nation.[245] His editorials in the *Baltimore Sun* had local as well as national followings, for Mencken had established himself as one of America's leading and most controversial writers.[246]

Mencken bemoaned the puritanical onslaught in America that caused the Eighteenth Amendment to become law in the first place.[247] He often called the era of Prohibition the "Methodist Millennium,"[248] and his dislike of the Methodists was evident in many of his columns throughout the Prohibition years. In March 1933, with the realization that beer would return, Mencken pondered how it was "amazing, looking backward, to contemplate the craven complaisance with which the American people endured the late Methodist tyranny."[249] Such contemptuous words were controversial in those times as much as they are today, but Mencken nevertheless enjoyed the controversy he stirred, as well as the resulting notoriety.

Despite his anger at those who brought about Prohibition, Mencken also expressed his anger at a docile American public that waited so long to fight the prohibitionists.[250] He noted, even as early as 1914, that the American people were the most "pusillanimous" race on earth because of their timidity in fighting the oppressive prohibitionists.[251] In 1920, Mencken stated that Prohibition *would* last because the wets were urban, unschooled, foolish politicians who would "succumb at the first onslaught, even to the first threat and the rural drys would support prohibition simply to gain votes."[252]

H.L. Mencken celebrates Prohibition's demise at the Hotel Rennert. *Maryland Historical Society, PVF. Permission from the Baltimore Sun Media Group.*

On April 7, 1933, it was not surprising at all (in fact, highly appropriate) that Mencken took center stage in the return of beer celebration in Baltimore, declaring the beer to be "pretty good, not bad at all. Fill it again," as he drank the first glass of beer (Baltimore's own Arrow beer) at the Old Rennert Hotel Bar.[253] In his editorial on April 10, Mencken used his column yet again as a voice against prohibitionists:

> *They were all set last Thursday night…with thousands of drunkards reeling down the streets and the gutters running blood, but what actually confronted them was a very decorous party, with so little of the unseemly in it that the cops had nothing to do. Here in Baltimore, touring the downtown hotels and cafes, I saw not the slightest sign of the predicted anarchy, save maybe among the sweating and demoralized bartenders.… The evening offered massive and overwhelming proof that 3.2% beer, taken in reasonable amounts, is not intoxicating.[254]*

Although he was overjoyed that beer had returned, he urged his readers to fight on and repeal the Eighteenth Amendment, which would bring back not only a higher alcohol percentage beer but also wines and liquor.[255] Mencken personally advocated a more German-tasting (as in German-style) 5 percent beer.[256]

Mencken's birthday was September 12. Coincidentally, September 12, 1933, was also the day on which Maryland elected its twenty-four wet delegates to a state convention that would ultimately repeal the Eighteenth Amendment. Of possibly even greater coincidence, it was also the eighty-eighth birthday of Joshua Levering, Maryland's presidential candidate of the Prohibition Party in the 1890s and early 1900s.[257] Mencken was overjoyed that his views finally seemed to have been vindicated by the popular vote. He did not hold a grudge against Mr. Levering, though. Mencken and Levering exchanged amicable greetings at the polls and hoped for each other's conversion.[258] Mencken used his sense of humor to

This is an autographed photograph of H.L. Mencken drinking a beer for breakfast in the Free State. *Wisconsin Historical Society, WHS 31913.*

say that he admired Levering and that "if all prohibitionists were as noble as he is, I'd sign the pledge (as for keeping it, that's another matter)."[259] Mencken remained true to his cause to the very end, never once faltering in his belief that Prohibition was a failed experiment.

AFRICAN AMERICANS

The history of African Americans' experiences during national Prohibition is not well chronicled in either primary or secondary historical documents.[260] Garrett Peck's examination of African Americans in Washington, D.C., is the one exception that intended to shed as much light as possible on this population's experience in a specific locale during Prohibition. The evidence and documents that do exist regarding the black experience with Prohibition reveal that much like other groups, African Americans' views on Prohibition were variable and susceptible to change. What historians Hanes Walton Jr. and James Taylor published in the journal *Phylon* in 1971 still holds remarkably true today: "It is difficult to ascertain the precise role of Blacks in the prohibition movement because of the rhetoric and conflicting viewpoint."[261] The African American experience in Baltimore and Maryland, a border state sharing qualities of both the North and the South, during the Prohibition era reveals such ambiguity toward the policy.

In 1910, Baltimore's black population was 84,749 (15.5 percent), in 1920 it was 108,322 (14.8 percent) and in 1930 it was 142,106 (17.7 percent).[262] New York City may have boasted the greatest absolute number of African Americans (91,709 in 1910, 152,467 in 1920 and 327,706 in 1930), but the "Big Apple" lagged far behind Baltimore in the black proportion to the city's total population (1.9 percent in 1910, 2.7 percent in 1920 and 4.7 percent in 1930 in New York City). According to the 1920 census, Maryland's African American population in 1920 totaled 244,479 men and women, about 16.8 percent of the total state population.[263] The 1930 census reveals that the African American population in Maryland swelled to 276,379, or 16.9 percent of the total state population.[264]

Perhaps because of these population numbers, Baltimore's African American population had a significant voice and public forum, at least for black citizens, in the *Baltimore Afro-American* newspaper. The *Afro-American* was the third largest African American newspaper in the United States and therefore provides the best, though limited, experiences and viewpoints of Prohibition by African Americans in Baltimore.[265]

There were some prominent African Americans who showed some support for prohibition policies during the 1910s. The Maryland Anti-Saloon League even established a "Colored Department" in 1912 at 1204 Druid Hill Avenue in west Baltimore City, with Reverend D. Dewitt Turpeau as department head from 1912 through 1915.[266] Turpeau was a minister in the African Methodist Episcopal Church, and as head of the department, he worked with the Maryland Anti-Saloon League to achieve local option laws throughout Maryland. His efforts were noted to be particularly successful in St. Mary's County, which opted to go dry in 1915.[267] The creation of the Colored Department by the Maryland ASL was supported by Booker T. Washington, who wrote the following to Maryland ASL superintendent W.H. Anderson:

> *By personal liberty and investigation that a very large part of the crime by colored men against white men and by white men against colored men has been committed under the influence of liquor. The Negro, more than any other element of our population has reason to be opposed to intemperance and where has a chance, as he has in Maryland, to vote for laws which will limit the evil, he should not fail to do so.*[268]

Historian Keith Vail noted that the Colored Department's efforts were supported by the Baltimore weekly newspaper the *Afro-American Ledger*, which remarked that the liquor traffic was "doing immense harm to the colored people of this country."[269] The creation of the Colored Department and the involvement of prominent clergymen like Turpeau from the AME Church does reveal that some African Americans in Baltimore and Maryland seemed to support alcohol prohibition policies. However, when Turpeau resigned from his position in 1915 to serve as pastor of the Simpson Methodist Church in Wheeling, West Virginia, little evidence exists to suggest that the Colored Department made any great contributions to the fight for constitutional Prohibition.[270]

In fact, there is only minimal information available that might show what African Americans in Baltimore and Maryland felt about the Eighteenth Amendment. The only evidence of noteworthy value leading up to the legal implementation of Prohibition was an editorial entitled "The King Is Dead," alluding to the fact that the patron saint of brewers, King Gambrinus, was soon to be "executed" by the implementation of the Volstead Act. The editorial begins by asserting that all those Americans who favored washing "the dust out of their throats" as part of family traditions would now have to travel to Canada, Cuba, Mexico or Europe:[271]

> *America, looking ahead and with vaunted democratic spirit of the age, has placed a ban on Kings, and the one that was most worshipped by the democratic hosts of its conglomerated population has had to go....* *King Alcohol was certainly among those who helped to fetter the colored people and was always opposed to their receiving justice in matters political and civil.*[272]

There is also little available evidence on the role of African Americans in bootlegging.[273] One piece that does exist is an article that appeared in the *Virginia Law Register* in September 1921. The author described the bootlegging industry as being inundated by the "Race Menace." The article states that the South and the larger cities on the Atlantic coast—specifically Baltimore, Philadelphia and Washington, D.C.—were believed to be in peril from the southern "Negroe bootleggers."[274] The article reveals a not unexpected condescending tone toward the African American population, particularly in the South. The article's author, Charles Hall Davis, stated that though he believes the majority of bootleggers in the South were "negroes," he does not mean to intimate that a large percentage of the black population were bootleggers, but rather just those who were low class and lawless.[275] The article reveals the anti-black prejudice of the period; however, it does provide evidence that some African Americans were involved in bootlegging operations or were at least openly defiant of the Volstead Act.

By 1933, the view of Prohibition held by the *Baltimore Afro-American* had seemingly undergone a marked change from one of support and/or indifference to the policy in the early 1920s to one of support for its repeal. After the experiences under Prohibition, particularly in Baltimore and Maryland, and also due to the economic impacts of the Depression, it is not altogether surprising that the *Afro-American* may have been more open to supporting repeal in 1933.

Repeal was now seen as a possible, but by no means guaranteed, opportunity for economic and psychological uplift for the African American community. An article during the week of April 1, 1933, hailed beer as the first sign of a coming prosperity that would alleviate the troubled times of the Great Depression and boost the clientele of restaurants and hotels in the Baltimore metropolitan area. Yet when the *Baltimore Afro-American* asked three African American women to give their thoughts on the return of beer, they seemed indifferent in their reactions.[276] Two of the women did not even offer an opinion, although they admitted that the prospect of repeal was a "vital" question.[277] The *Afro-American* reported that the one woman who did comment stated that the effect of repeal "will depend on how it is dispensed. It can be reduced to a very debauching condition if not properly handled."[278]

Although there was a common apprehension about an expensive excess tax on beer in the city, some managers and owners of these African American–operated restaurants and hotels seemed willing to pay the tax, believing that the increase in customers would produce an overall profit. Samuel Keys, the manager of the Penn Hotel (the first African American–owned hotel in Baltimore, established in 1921), planned on building a beer garden, believing that the return of beer and light wines would "be a boon to Baltimore."[279] Clifton Monroe, who owned Cliff's Restaurant on Druid Hill Avenue and Orchard Street, declared that he would sell beer and was optimistic about an upswing in his business, stating that "there is nothing like a cold mug of beer along with an appetizing meal on a warm summer's day."[280]

One final piece of evidence that indicates that the African American community likely welcomed the return of beer was the fact that more than two thousand black Baltimoreans gathered on Pennsylvania Avenue (the cultural and commercial center for Baltimore's African Americans) to celebrate the end of Prohibition at midnight on April 7, 1933.[281] Thousands in Baltimore's African American community celebrated the return of beer just as white folks did—with pomp and circumstance and a glass of beer held firmly in hand. In moments such as those, even in 1930s Baltimore, the color of one's skin was negligible as most Baltimoreans rejoiced.

Chapter 4

"FREE STATE" ECONOMICS AND
PUBLIC HEALTH DEBATES

I n 1920, the Maryland Board of Labor and Statistics published its *Twenty-Ninth Annual Report*, which revealed some of the economic impact of Prohibition on sections of Maryland's economy during its first year of implementation:

> *The Volstead act in 1920 cost Maryland $1,069,710.02 in liquor license fees, exclusive of bottlers' taxes In 1919 the clerk's office collected $1,070,226.69 from liquor licenses, compared to $516.67 in 1920. The bulk of the loss occurred through elimination of 914 of the common variety of corner saloon, which contributed $953,400 in 1919 and nothing in 1920. Other complete losses were 23 hotel licenses, at $1,000 each; 18 hotels of not more than 200 rooms, totaling $4,500; five small hotels, totaling $2,500; 12 retail grocers' liquor licenses, $6,000; 14 clubs, $10,500; 23 ordinaries, $5,860. In 1918, 58 wholesale liquor dealers paid $52,716.69 and seven wholesale druggists, $1,750. The Tax Court reported a decrease of $300,000 in the distilled spirits in bond basis, amounting to a loss in revenue of $8,910 in the old city, and $13,305.60 in the new Annex, where the decrease in basis was $700,000. This makes a total loss in revenue of $22,215.60, due to prohibition.*[282]

Perhaps the most obvious cost of Prohibition was the economic impact that the Eighteenth Amendment had on certain businesses, particularly those that dealt in liquor manufacturing and distribution. Prohibition essentially shuttered these businesses and/or reduced or terminated prior trading partners and channels (particularly with foreign nations that extensively traded in America's water ports like Baltimore).[283]

AN INDUSTRY IN SHAMBLES

Baltimore and Maryland were areas where the liquor industry had an established economic presence in the community. In 1905, there were 4,200 saloons in Maryland. Of those, 2,200 were in Baltimore City.[284] By 1913, thanks to the efforts of the ASL, that number had been reduced to fewer than 1,500 in Baltimore.[285] By July 1920, most of the bars and saloons in Baltimore had closed.[286] Many of the bars, hotels and converted saloons that remained open on Baltimore's streets sold only soft drinks.[287] Other former saloonkeepers and bar owners either outright closed their businesses or resorted to speakeasies and bootleg liquor.

A November 1, 1908 picture shows a typical (but unidentified) Baltimore saloon and bartender in the early twentieth century. *Photo by John Dubas Baltimore City Life Museum Collection, Maryland Historical Society, MC9205.*

City hotels—such as the Emerson Hotel, the Hotel Rennert, Belvedere Hotel and Lord Baltimore Hotel—faced major revenue shortfalls, as hotels made much of their profits from bar sales.[288] It was estimated that Baltimore hotels held at least $1 million in stocks of wet goods. With Prohibition's arrival nearly a month away, hotels in major American cities including New York, Boston, Philadelphia and Baltimore met with the House Agricultural Committee because the hotels in these cities and others had huge cash investments in liquor stocks that would become "dead losses" once Prohibition was enacted on January 20, 1920.[289] Without the hotel bar, the value of the hotels' properties decreased. With the onset of Prohibition, the industry turned its attention (and some of the physical space and property facilities) toward establishing restaurants as part of these sites. Despite the fact that hotels gained some new customers throughout the Prohibition years, the competition from the burgeoning speakeasies and nightclubs in the 1920s kept those planned prospective revenues from their restaurants in check.[290]

Before Prohibition was enacted, Maryland boasted a total of twenty-nine breweries. Of that number, twenty-three were situated in Baltimore, a concentration largely owing to the city's central location in the state and its significant German American population.[291] Of the eleven Baltimore breweries that reopened in 1933, many were under new management and/or ownership. By the mid-1960s, only six of the eleven breweries from 1933 remained in operation. The six remaining began to die off just as national breweries like Anheuser-Busch and Pabst flooded the market, especially from the late 1950s through the 1980s. Along with business consolidation within the brewing industry after 1933, there is no doubt that Prohibition was one of the main culprits in precipitating the decline of Baltimore's brewing industry in the mid- to late twentieth century.

Ironically, in the late 1800s and early 1900s, beer was actually being marketed as a temperance drink. Breweries and the United States Brewers' Association marketed beer as "liquid bread" and as a light alternative to distilled spirits like whiskey.[292] In the early twentieth century, beer was rising in popularity at the expense of distilled spirits. An important reason for this was the burgeoning growth of American cities, where beer developed into the primary drink of choice.[293] It was in part because of this market rivalry that the distilling and brewing industries could not conceive a cooperative political strategy to battle prohibitionists.[294] Beer was a lighter beverage than distilled liquors, and thus there was reasonable thought and even expectation that Prohibition laws would not include beer.

Captain Isaac Emerson's Bromo-Seltzer Tower, 1930. Emerson was a Baltimore resident responsible for developing Bromo-Seltzer, a medicine that could alleviate headaches. Bromo-Seltzer was likely consumed by defiant Baltimoreans during Prohibition as a remedy for hangovers. *Baltimore Museum of Industry, Baltimore Gas & Electric Company Photographic Collection, BGE.4202.*

Baltimore and Maryland's distilling industry had a stellar reputation for producing fine rye whiskey prior to Prohibition, as Maryland fell behind only Kentucky and Pennsylvania in producing the nation's whiskey.[295] Between 1865 and 1917, Maryland Rye "commanded national respect" and was "on par with whatever else might be nominated as *ne plus ultra* of American whiskey."[296] Just about thirty Maryland distilleries were in operation as late as

Left: Captain Emerson's Emerson Hotel, with its ubiquitous hotel bar, was just one of the many hotels in Baltimore that experienced economic troubles due to Prohibition. *Baltimore Museum of Industry, Baltimore Gas & Electric Company Photographic Collection, BGE.4207.*

Below: A 2017 photo of Melvale Distillery's stone building, one of the last remaining pre-Prohibition structures related to Maryland's rich distilling history. Today, it is home to a vinegar plant. *Michael T. Walsh.*

An advertisement for the popular Melvale Distillery, located at 1900 Brand Avenue (right near Cold Spring Lane and the Jones Falls). *Baltimore Museum of Industry, Baltimore Gas & Electric Company Photographic Collection, BGE.40.S.*

1910.[297] The initiation of local option laws throughout Maryland's counties in the early 1900s and, finally, Prohibition itself decimated Maryland's whiskey industry and reputation. Only in very recent years has Maryland, through fairly small craft distilleries, really begun a comeback in producing rye whiskies.

Despite the general belief that beer would be spared from constitutional Prohibition, the brewing industry in Baltimore still paid for a prominent full-page ad in the February 5, 1918 edition of the *Sun* in which the brewers stated their belief that they had "failed to discover a single Maryland newspaper which has advocated the ratification of the Constitutional Amendment without submitting it to the vote of the people."[298] Excerpted editorials from the *Sun*, *Rockville Sentinel*, *Frederick Post* and other newspapers seemed to support the brewers' argument. The next day, another ad appeared that was addressed to the General Assembly of Maryland. This ad's language bears a resemblance to the brewers' advertisement from the day before and thus was presumably also paid for by the brewers, although the ad was attributed to no one in particular. The ad, a blatant appeal to states' rights, noted the following:

> *This is the Question the Public Asks You: Your OATH is binding, on your Conscience. Do you intend to violate it by voting to ratify the National Prohibition Amendment, thereby surrendering the Police Power of the State to the Federal Government, without submitting such amendment of the Constitution of Maryland to the qualified voters of the State, as is obligatory under the Constitution which you have sworn to support?*

Next to this ad was an advertisement in response to the brewers' initial ad. Fifteen county newspapers—including the *Kent News* (Kent County), *The Advance* (Dorchester County) and *The Herald* (Carroll County)—concluded that the brewers had been mistaken because they, in fact, promoted their newspapers as supporters of the national Prohibition amendment.[299] In a large front-page advertisement in the *Sun* on February 7, 1918, twenty-one more county newspapers also countered the brewers' belief that no newspapers in Maryland seemed to support the national Prohibition amendment.[300] A subsequent listing of Maryland newspapers appeared (mostly small and community oriented) that were in favor of Prohibition. None of the newspapers was located in Baltimore or Baltimore County.

The *Baltimore Sun* interviewed Albert H. Wehr, president of the Gottlieb-Bauernschmidt-Straus Brewing Company, in response to Dr. Heisse's comments regarding the possibility of a national Prohibition policy.[301] Wehr was optimistic even at that late date that the wets would persevere. Other Baltimore brewers, speaking anonymously, expressed doubt that the wets would win the battle either in Maryland or on the national level, but they also agreed that they had time to figure out what to do with their companies.[302] There would be, they thought, a seven-year period needed for the states to ratify the amendment. Breweries that failed to convert to another form of production (such as malt syrup, an ingredient often used for homebrew) or had decided not to close their facilities began to produce "near beer," which involved making real beer and then reducing its alcoholic content to the legal limit. One Baltimore brewery worker had supposed that his company would probably venture into the "near beer" business because Washington, D.C., had already been "doing a very large business in 'near beer.'"[303] For comparative purposes, the "near beer" of yesteryear would most closely resemble the alcohol content contained in non-alcoholic beer on the market today.

On July 1, 1919, the brewers gained what seemed to be the significant advantage that would enable them to continue the manufacture and distribution of beer. The Wartime Prohibition Act had stated that the manufacture and distribution of beer would be outlawed effective June 30, 1919. However, the United States District Court in Maryland, headed by Judge John Carter Rose, ruled to allow the sale of 2.75 percent beer.[304] The case centered on the fact that the Standard Brewing Company in Baltimore had produced beer that contained 0.5 percent alcohol. According to the Volstead Act, alcohol by volume could not be or exceed 0.5 percent alcohol by volume. Therefore, Standard Brewing was indicted. Judge Rose based his decision on a precedent established in a similar New York case that was then pending in the Supreme Court, a case that had allowed New York brewers to continue to manufacture 2.75 percent beer. Judge Rose also stated that the exact definition of the word *intoxicating*, defined by Congress in the Volstead Act, would not be clear until the Supreme Court's ruling.[305] Until a Supreme Court decision was rendered, Judge Rose said that Baltimore's brewers could produce beer up to 2.75 percent but risked being indicted again if the Supreme Court decided that 2.75 percent beer was intoxicating. This initial victory turned out to be fleeting, for in December 1919, the Supreme Court ruled that even 2.75 percent would be outlawed under the rules, statutes and enforcement of Prohibition, effective January 1920.

BALTIMORE'S BREWERIES

Recent additions to Baltimore's brewing history—Maureen O' Prey's *Brewing in Baltimore* and Rob Kasper's *Baltimore Beer: A Satisfying History of Charm City Brewing*—have both provided valuable insight into the city's strong brewing history and how Prohibition affected Baltimore's breweries. However, it is William J. Kelley's book *Brewing in Maryland*, written in 1965, that still provides the best historical evidence and records, incomplete as they may be, of what happened to some of Baltimore's breweries because of national Prohibition.

One of the more renowned breweries in Baltimore by 1920, owing in large part to its well-known bottled product G-B-S Special ($1.25 per case), was the Globe Brewery.[306] The Globe, on South Hanover Street, was founded in 1888 by German Americans Frederick Gottlieb, Frederick Bauernschmidt and William Straus, whose G-B-S Brewing Company operated several

Three pre-Prohibition beer bottles. The two clear bottles are from Fred Bauernschmidt's American Brewery; the amber bottle is from the Gottlieb-Bauernschmidt-Straus Brewing Company. *Author's collection, Michael T. Walsh.*

Baltimore breweries until the company began to liquidate its assets in 1919. The Globe was then purchased by the Boston Iron and Metal Company, which became the first Baltimore brewery to produce "near beer," branded Arrow Special. After several years, the company began to increase the distribution range and gradually improve the taste of Arrow Special, as consumers nostalgically bought the beverage that was the closest approximation to pre-Prohibition beer.[307] Once it was learned that "real" beer was to return in April 1933, the Globe, under assistant brew master John J. Fitzgerald, was bestowed the "honor, distinction and extreme pleasure" of producing the first beer in Baltimore.[308] More than sixty trucks sped out of the Globe's parking lot to distribution destinations on April 7, 1933.[309]

Gunther's Brewery, located on South Conkling Street, produced one of Baltimore's most popular beers and one of its most durable. George Gunther Sr. was a German American whose family business was the brewery. After his death in 1912, his two sons, George Jr. and Frank H. Gunther, became heads of Gunther's Brewery and were in charge in January 1920. In 1919, the George Gunther Jr. Brewing Company became the George Gunther Jr. Manufacturing Company. This reorganization allowed the plant to produce ice and "near beer." By 1923, sales of "near beer" were plummeting, so ice production was drastically increased. Nonetheless, the brewery was heavily in debt by the early 1930s. William J. Kelley suggested that the Gunther brothers' downfall was their obstinate refusal to stop production of the unpopular "near beer." With Frank's death in 1931, the company was put under receivership, and the brewery and its assets came under the control of Abraham Krieger. Under Krieger, Gunther's Brewery became the second brewery to produce real beer in the city in 1933, and the brewery did enjoy years of prosperity after Prohibition.

The American Brewery was founded in 1863 as the John F. Wiessner & Sons Brewing Company at 1700 North Gay Street. The Wiessner family

Above: The Globe Brewery in full operation in 1938, five years after the end of Prohibition. *Baltimore Museum of Industry, Baltimore Gas & Electric Company Photographic Collection, BGE.11894.*

Left: Located at 1211 South Conkling Street in Baltimore's Canton neighborhood, Gunther's Brewery (here pictured in February 1934) was one of Baltimore's most successful breweries before and after Prohibition. *Baltimore Museum of Industry, Baltimore Gas & Electric Company Photographic Collection, BGE.7833.*

The American Malt Company in August 1931. This High-Victorian Gothic building, located at 1700 North Gay Street, was the J.F. Wiessner & Sons Brewing Company prior to Prohibition; after repeal, it was rebranded as the American Brewery. *Baltimore Museum of Industry, Baltimore Gas & Electric Company Photographic Collection, BGE.5268N.*

operated a rather successful business in Baltimore until Prohibition arrived, producing a peak of about 110,000 barrels of beer per year in 1919.[310] In 1920, the American Brewery stopped production of alcoholic beer. At that time, there were sixty-one total workers at the American Brewery plant—"16 in brewerywork, 17 drivers, 14 in the bottling house, 8 garage men, and 6 office workers" (records indicating workforce numbers for "near beer" production are not available).[311] The brewery soon stopped all production of even "near beer" and "went into mothballs with just a skeleton force on hand for maintenance."[312]

In 1926, the Fitzsimmons family, under the guidance of John Fitzsimmons, bought the brewery from the Wiessner estate and formed the American Malt Company, which produced malt syrup.[313] Fitzsimmons anticipated the repeal of Prohibition in 1931 by buying several old breweries at a cheap price, and he consolidated all of the brewing equipment into the Wiessner plant.[314] As the prospect of repeal came closer, the *Baltimore Post* remarked that the statue of King Gambrinus in front of the brewery began to smile.[315] On July 12, 1933, the brewery made its first deliveries of beer and changed

The statue of King Gambrinus, known to be the patron saint of beers, stood guard at the American Brewery. The statue now resides in the Maryland Historical Society. *Baltimore Museum of Industry, Baltimore Gas & Electric Company Photographic Collection, BGE.9.C.*

its name to the American Brewery Inc. The American Brewery remained in business until 1973.

George Brehm & Sons Brewery, located then on Belair Avenue in northeast Baltimore, managed to remain in business throughout Prohibition by converting its business to soda production. This conversion allowed the brewery to operate on a legal business throughout Prohibition, although rumors and legends persist to this day that a bootleg tunnel from the brewery—to the nearby Seidel's Duckpin Bowling Alley (located on the major commercial and easily accessible thoroughfare, Belair Road)—existed for transport of beer the brewery was still illegally producing.[316] In 1933, the brewery returned to beer but was later bought in 1935 by the Burton Brewing Company, which soon went into receivership in 1940.[317]

Theodore Reichart, from Bavaria, originally served as head of cellar operations in John F. Wiessner & Sons Brewing Company from 1907 to 1920. In 1930, he began to purchase machinery for a plant on Harford Road in Baltimore, the Reichart Brewery. Reichart then proceeded, illegally, to produce real beer out of the plant (the plant itself was valued at $100,000),

Inside the American Malt Company in August 1932. It is possible that the company had already begun at least a partial reconversion back to beer production in this plant to be ready for imminent repeal. *Baltimore Museum of Industry, Baltimore Gas & Electric Company Photographic Collection, BGE.5268.*

at a rate of 1,500 to 2,000 gallons of beer per day.[318] On August 17, 1931, Prohibition agents raided his plant, and the equipment and plant were destroyed. This did not stop Reichart. By the spring and summer of 1933, Reichart had begun equipping a new brewery at 2208 Harford Road, and by November, production had commenced. Unfortunately for Reichart, the years following the end of Prohibition could not match the initial euphoria and profits of the months immediately following repeal. In 1937, with profits stagnant partly due to the lingering Depression, the brewery was taken over by the Chesapeake Brewing Corporation. Reichart remained as brew master, but the business was no longer his own.

When President Roosevelt asked Congress to amend the Volstead Act to allow 3.2 percent beer in March 1933, many brewers in Baltimore wasted little time in an attempt to produce and market this newly legal beer. Carl Brohmeyer, the former brew master of J.F. Wiessner & Sons Brewing Company, hinted that 3 percent beer would be "pretty good."[319]

The American Brewery produced beer until 1973. It was recently renovated as a social services center and remains one of the most interesting architectural buildings in Baltimore. *Michael T. Walsh.*

The last remaining building of George Brehm and Sons Brewery (3501 Brehm's Lane), pictured here in 2017, in northeast Baltimore (present-day Belair-Edison neighborhood). *Michael T. Walsh.*

This assessment was also given by another former brew master, Mr. Eugene Schroyer, who noted that many pre-Prohibition Baltimore beers were around 3 percent as well.[320] Mr. Fritz Baum, owner of German restaurant Café Baum at 320 West Saratoga Street, said he would reserve his judgment until he tasted the first shipment, although he fully anticipated serving the new beer at his restaurant regardless of taste due to popular demand.[321] With the anticipated return of a good-tasting beer, the bartenders' union became reactivated, and the local brewers' union in Baltimore (which never disbanded) once again formed divisions among its brewers, bottlers, drivers and engineers.[322]

The demand for beer in Baltimore was expected to be high with the end of Prohibition. Gunther's Brewery president Abraham Krieger stated that the company had employed an additional three hundred men three weeks before April 7 and then added two hundred more men on April 6 (an exact workforce figure, however, remains unknown).[323] In the weeks leading up to beer's return to Baltimore, the Globe Brewery advertised that its brewery would remain open all night on April 6 and 7, and it introduced a new slogan for its franchise Arrow beer and Arrow Bock beer: "Good in '17, Better Today."[324] On April 6, Gunther's Brewery also advertised in the *Evening Sun*, telling its patrons to "Stand By: Uncle Sam's Official Time-Keepers Will Release GUNTHER'S REAL BEER ONE MINUTE AFTER MIDNIGHT."[325]

On April 7, at 12:05 a.m., one hundred Gunther beer trucks rolled out of the brewery grounds to deliver the new beer to Baltimore and other counties in the state. About one thousand spectators were on hand, hoping that the rumor of free beer was true.[326] The rumor proved to be false, but the people still reacted enthusiastically. At the Globe Brewery, twenty-five patrolmen were on the site to control the enormous number of people who lined the streets near the brewery.[327] The government inspector called time even though the watches of the brewery workers showed that it was only 11:50 p.m.[328] The trucks left by the dozens from the Globe to deliver its product to Baltimore. The next day, the Globe Brewery ran an ad that thanked Baltimore and Maryland for their support in the return of beer:

> *We thank Baltimore and Maryland for their amazing support of Arrow Beer. Everybody had one thing on their minds—Beer—Real Beer—Foaming Beer—ARROW BEER. Customers stormed the Globe Brewery all night long. We did the best we could, but no amount of planning or foresight could have stemmed the tide. If any one's order was missed—we're sorry. We'll keep right on working—night and day until every order is filled. Thank you again! Signed—THE GLOBE BREWERY*[329]

By Sunday, April 9, most of Baltimore's breweries had run out of beer and did not expect to make any more deliveries until Tuesday, April 11! The doors were locked and the blinds were drawn at Gunther's Brewery.[330] Clerks outside took future orders but not orders for immediate delivery.[331] One month after the return of beer, strong demand persisted for the beer.[332] In July 1933, it was reported that the sale of beer had given the city of Baltimore $175,000 in revenue, which ranked near the top of the list of municipal revenues generated by the return of beer.[333]

In the short term, the initial return of beer to Baltimore was a success. New breweries sprouted in Baltimore, and old breweries under new management, in particular the National Brewing Company (first founded in 1872), now reopened for business. National Brewing Company, now owned by the German American Hoffberger family, incorporated and moved to a new facility in Canton, where it became the beer most associated with Baltimore in the latter half of the twentieth century due to its branding of the iconic Mr. Boh logo and memorable tagline that called the Chesapeake region the "Land of Pleasant Living" on every bottle and can of its beer.[334]

However, Baltimore's pre-Prohibition brewing industry never fully recovered. The return of beer after Prohibition also involved the growing

The National Brewing Company (Conkling at O'Donnell Street in Canton). Although no longer brewed in Baltimore, "Natty Boh" remains a popular beer among Baltimoreans today. *Michael T. Walsh.*

trend toward big corporate beer manufacturers and distributors and corporate consolidations of smaller breweries into larger macrobreweries (for example, Standard Brewing Company, brewers of Bismarch beer in Baltimore, was bought by Croft Brewing of New York, and the announcement was made in a huge ad in the *New York Times* on July 17, 1933).[335] The remaining breweries in Baltimore never fully adjusted to a different, more corporate and cutthroat brewing industry after repeal, and they lacked the capital to compete with the large breweries (like Anheuser-Busch and Miller Brewing) that were going national from the 1940s through the early 1970s. The proliferation and success of craft microbreweries in the city and state since the mid-1990s began a revitalization of Baltimore and Maryland's brewing industry after several lost generations. Finally, in the 2010s, the brewing industry in Baltimore and Maryland is thriving locally and regionally nearly a century after Prohibition incapacitated that industry.

OTHER INDUSTRIES: COSTS AND BENEFITS

Once it was clear that Prohibition would become a reality, leading American chemists—major employees of the industrial alcohol business—realized that Prohibition would severely affect their field of work, and meetings of the American Chemical Society were held in New York, Philadelphia and Baltimore to discuss and form a uniform reaction to the Volstead Act.[336] Chemists were greatly displeased with the vagueness of the law, which they felt might lead to inefficiencies in manufacturing (due to the inability to obtain high-grade products for their work) and distribution of their products. Baltimore was home to one of the major industrial alcohol plants in America, U.S. Industrial Alcohol (USIA) in the Curtis Bay neighborhood. USIA, which itself was sanctioned and approved by the federal government, was one of the leading producers of alcohol that could be used for both industrial and medicinal purposes. At a 1921 speech in Rumford Hall in New York, USIA vice-president Dr. M.C. Whitaker stated that Prohibition enforcement officials "are totally lacking in knowledge of its industrial relations to chemical industry, to their home comforts, to the health of themselves and their families, to the progress of science and to national defense."[337]

Whitaker did provide two examples of why he felt the enforcement of Prohibition in his industry was folly and impeded the business of the industry. He noted a preposterous example in which the general counsels of telephone companies in Boston and Baltimore advised U.S. Industrial Alcohol that its listing in the telephone directory would be illegal under the Volstead Act. USIA had to obtain a special ruling from Washington to enable it to keep its corporate title in the telephone book.[338] In another example, on May 15, 1920, in Baltimore, the U.S. Chemical Company delivered thirty-two drums to a steamship bound for France. The agents on the ship could not accept the cargo because the word alcohol appeared on the drums and on the bill of landing. This forced the drums to be "reloaded, trucked back to the plant...relabeled and new bills-of-landing prepared under the name 'Iso-butyl Solvent,' and the steamship company finally relented and accepted the very legal cargo for transportation across the Atlantic Ocean."[339]

Although the USIA plant in Baltimore had to contend with the potential negative effects as a result of Prohibition, one can also make the case that the company profited from the passage of the policy. Although the plant in Curtis Bay was one of the leading producers of legal industrial alcohol throughout the Prohibition period, it was also one of the leading producers of bootleg liquor, renaturing the product in an attempt to make the industrial alcohol drinkable.[340] Baltimore's harbor provided access not only for incoming bootleg liquor but also for outgoing bootleg alcohol, courtesy of USIA. Federal agents once discovered eight thousand gallons of bootleg USIA grain alcohol waiting for export at President Street Station in Baltimore covertly labeled as "olive oil."[341]

Of course, there were benefits to the economy due to the policy of national Prohibition as well. The Baltimore & Ohio Railroad Company was one Baltimore business that offered its support of Prohibition in the *Manufacturer's Record*. Baltimore & Ohio vice-president C.W. Galloway wrote that he noticed "an improvement in this condition [operation and maintenance at the plant] with respect to the number of employees dismissed for violation of the rule pertaining to drinking."[342] Not surprisingly, Henry S. Dulaney, treasurer of Maryland's ASL and co-founder of the Resinol Chemical Company, offered his support of Prohibition in the *Manufacturer's Record*, saying that "I am quite sure that the effect of Prohibition on the laboring man cannot be anything but for his betterment."[343]

Some entrepreneurs attempted to capitalize on Prohibition. One such example was offered by Arthur Hodges of Baltimore, who filed an application

An aerial overview of the sprawling United States Industrial Alcohol plant in Curtis Bay that produced industrial and bootleg alcohol during Prohibition. *Baltimore Museum of Industry, Baltimore Gas & Electric Company Photographic Collection, BGE.11941.*

on January 30, 1923, with the U.S. Patent Office for "improvements in game apparatus."[344] Hodges had created a Prohibition board game, with the object being to move the gaming pieces (checkers) around the board by spinning a numbered wheel, with the starting point being labeled as WCTU, through the various states of the Union represented on the board. The first player to reach the square labeled Eighteenth Amendment would win the game!

THE HEALTH HAZARDS OF ALCOHOL

Recent studies by scholars of Prohibition have emphasized that the demonizing of alcohol was a "fight against a genuine public health malady."[345] Alcohol consumption was contributing to an increase in liver cirrhosis (15 per 100,000 total population).[346] Alcohol use and alcoholism (10 per 100,000 adult population) were believed to have played vital contributing roles in the escalation of domestic abuse; of home, job and school delinquency; of early death; and of increasing physical and mental ailments—all of which had to be handled by the healthcare professionals of the day.[347]

Some scholars have argued that annual public consumption of alcohol did indeed decrease as a result of Prohibition and that consumption did not reach the pre-Prohibition "high water mark" until well after repeal. Divorces granted on account of alcoholism fell by 52 percent as divorces for all other causes increased.[348] Deaths from liver cirrhosis also declined sharply, as did patient admissions into mental hospitals.[349] A study performed as late as 1932 aimed at gathering statistics from the state mental hospitals of nineteen states (Maryland was not among them) offered evidence that the intemperate use of alcohol contributed to alcoholic mental disease/psychoses.[350]

Despite the apparent benefits of national Prohibition for public health, there were also corresponding costs and unintended consequences. Among the important unintended consequences of enacting Prohibition were the afflictions and fatalities that occurred due to imbibing poisonous alcohol.[351] Often generalized and referred to as "bathtub gin" or "hooch," potent and poisonous alcohol—frequently a result of homemade concoctions in hidden stills or bathtubs or the consumption of industrial-strength alcohol—led to a great many ailments and deaths in America. Some of these concoctions were based on shoe polish and cologne.[352] Representative John Linthicum of Maryland argued that 10 percent of all industrial alcohol had been leaking into beverage channels since Prohibition began and that there were 11,700 deaths in 1926 due to poisonous alcohol.[353] Linthicum proposed an anti-poison bill that aimed at "prohibiting poison denaturants in industrial alcohol."[354] The amendment was voted on in the House of Representatives but was defeated 283-61, with 89 members not voting and 91 absent from the vote.[355] By 1927, the U.S. government, led by the Treasury Department, had ordered industrial alcohol companies to insert, as part of the denaturing process, an often lethal cocktail of chemicals into their alcohol, including such chemicals as gasoline, kerosene, chloroform and, most significantly, methyl alcohol.[356] Once the industrial alcohol was bootlegged, the renatured alcohol still contained chemicals that would prove greatly harmful when consumed.[357] Scholars today continue to struggle with the morality of the federal government's decision in demanding the insertion of the new potentially lethal chemicals in industrial alcohol, knowing that it might be consumed and cause illness and death.[358]

In 1921, a loose coalition of brewers, chemists and physicians attempted to convince Congress and Attorney General A. Mitchell Palmer of the curative value of beer and alcohol. Medical practitioners realized just how much harm alcohol use could do to one's health but also knew that "it is a valuable drug, when judiciously employed in certain diseases."[359] In November 1921, Congress took up the issue of medicinal beer with the Willis-Campbell bill (passed in the House by a vote of 250-93 and in the Senate by a 39-20 vote), which legislated that beer could not be used for medicinal purposes and also limited wine and liquor prescriptions to "not more than a half pint in ten days."[360] The Willis-Campbell Act made enforcement even stricter but did confirm that industrial alcohol was exempt from the Volstead law.

By the end of the 1920s, however, even the success of Prohibition in the medical field was being chastised by reputable sources. In 1929, at the eightieth convention of the American Medical Association (AMA) in Portland, Baltimore physician and AMA president William Sydney Thayer put a "valedictory damnation" on legislation that governs "what we may or may not eat or drink, as to how we may dress, as to our religious beliefs or as to what we may or may not read."[361] *TIME* reported that his "general denunciation" of such legislation was generally seen as an attack against Prohibition."[362] *TIME* reported, not without tongue firmly planted in cheek, that the consensus of the convention was that Prohibition "baffles medical practice, that alcoholics are at times a medical necessity."[363]

JOHNS HOPKINS HOSPITAL AND UNIVERSITY

In Baltimore and Maryland, much of the evidence related to public health and Prohibition comes from one of the most well-regarded institutions in the world: Johns Hopkins Hospital and University. As with any institution of substantial size and influence, there were many differing viewpoints among the employees of the Johns Hopkins University and the Johns Hopkins Hospital.

A few examples of proponents and opponents of Prohibition at Johns Hopkins reveal the disparity of views on the issue and the ramifications it had on health and society. Dr. Adolph Meyer had been the psychiatrist-in-chief since 1909 of the Johns Hopkins Hospital and was generally known to be a supporter of temperance and Prohibition. A man who had made major and pioneering contributions to the field of psychiatry and mental hygiene,[364] Dr. Meyer used his medical background and research with alcohol psychoses and neurology to reach certain conclusions about alcohol and the need for alcohol regulation in order to promote healthy mental hygiene. Dr. Meyer was often quoted by prohibitionists, who used his research to substantiate their claims about the dangers of excessive alcohol use. Dr. Meyer presented those conclusions best in his essay "Alcohol as a Psychiatric Problem," which appeared in Dr. Haven Emerson's edited 1932 book *Alcohol and Man* and in Ferdinand Iglehart's *King Alcohol Dethroned*. Meyer recognized "the desire for more" alcohol, in essence recognizing alcohol addiction as a great peril and a cause of potential deterioration of the human nervous system (as opposed to seeing alcohol as merely a vice).[365] Such a statement revealed the shift away from the popular turn-of-the-century Keeley Cure (established by Dr. Leslie Keeley), in which patients afflicted with alcoholism were given injections of gold chloride, and toward an enlightened and scientific exploration into what might make a person yearn for intoxicating substances. Just as with many social and health reformers of his day, Meyer also felt that alcoholism was a problem of "entire groups, and not merely the individual."[366]

Dr. Howard Atwood Kelly was a Baltimore surgeon and gynecologist who gained much prestige at Johns Hopkins and who was a known supporter of Prohibition.[367] In the waning days of 1932, with President-elect Franklin D. Roosevelt waiting in the wings with his and his party's platform of repeal and an immediate proposal to bring about beer's return, women drys lobbied the Ways and Means Committee in Washington, D.C., in an attempt to fight the Collier beer bill, which aimed to return the sale of light beer. Mrs. Henry

The Johns Hopkins Hospital Henry Phipps Psychiatric Clinic, built in 1912. The prestigious hospital was home to both opponents and proponents of Prohibition. *Michael T. Walsh.*

W. Peabody, who was head of the Women's National Committee on Law Enforcement, used Dr. Kelly's judgment that "one half of 1 percent is the safe limit for alcohol beverages."[368] Dr. Kelly, in fact, had once stated before a WCTU conference in Washington, D.C., that "most doctors would be glad to be rid of the privilege of prescribing liquor of any kind."[369] In March 1933, almost immediately after the Blaine bill was signed by President Roosevelt, signaling the return of beer to many regions of America, Kelly, along with Drs. William Howell and E.V. McCollum of Johns Hopkins, asserted that 2.75 percent beer was indeed intoxicating and that a move to 3.2 percent beer would be even worse.[370]

One of the leading opponents of Prohibition at Johns Hopkins University was a well-respected historian. Dr. John Holladay Latane was professor of American history in the Walter Hines Page School of International Relations at Johns Hopkins University, heading that department from 1913 until his death in 1932, and served as dean from 1919 to 1924.[371] Latane was clearly aggravated by Prohibition and made a bold prediction (for the time) that Prohibition would be "dead letters or repealed within thirty years."[372] In fact, he made some rather incendiary remarks in his lifetime, including expressing his predisposition to throw a bomb in the cellar of the building in Washington, D.C., that housed the office of the Board of Temperance, Prohibition and Public Morals of the Methodist Episcopal Church.[373] In 1928, Dr. Latane, in an address to the Young People's Democratic League, fully endorsed Al Smith's campaign for the presidency.[374] Latane was even part of Smith's welcome committee to

Baltimore at Johns Hopkins in October 1928 as the presidential candidate made his last round of campaign stops before the election.[375]

In a final example, Dr. Esther Loring Richards was an associate professor of psychiatry at Johns Hopkins University and a lecturer at the School of Hygiene and Public Health in Baltimore. In April 1931, the *New York Times* reported that Dr. Richards had publicly proclaimed her opposition to Prohibition and had joined Pauline Sabin's Women's Organization for National Prohibition Reform because of her experiences and observations in her professional and private life.[376] Her aim was to make Prohibition—which she deemed to be "psychologically unsound," "intellectually dishonest" and "mistaken legislation"—into an "adjunct to temperate living."[377] Dr. Richards noted that public morale was at an all-time low, most notably because of the Depression, and argued that Prohibition and the reported ills of the legislation were both adding to the perception that the law was ineffective and adding to the lack of public optimism and the American spirit.[378]

Chapter 5

CRIME IN JAZZ AGE BALTIMORE

A uthor and scholar Carl Bode has written that "the 1920s, our last great Age of Euphoria, arrived in Maryland carrying a hip flask, dancing the fox-trot, and dressing on credit, all at the same time."[379] An establishment that boasted a red hard crab sign outside its restaurant meant to those in the know that it provided seafood as well as real beer.[380] Crain Highway was even unofficially rechristened as "Bootleg Boulevard" (perhaps not coincidentally, present-day Crain Highway merges with Ritchie Highway, named after Maryland's famous wet governor).

The apparent increase of criminal activity was without a doubt the great unintended consequence of national Prohibition. When the Eighteenth Amendment was implemented, legislators could not have predicted how a constitutional amendment—aimed at reducing and if possible ending excessive alcohol consumption, which often manifested itself in violent behavior—would help to usher in a new era of criminal and violent behavior because of the *absence* of commercial and readily available alcohol.

Table 6 contains figures compiled by Isidor "Izzie" Einstein, one of the most prominent agents of the Prohibition Unit (or Bureau of Prohibition), and given to *Time* magazine in 1923.[381] It calculates the amount of time Einstein had to wait upon arrival at each destination, in order to obtain a drink in major U.S. cities. In New Orleans, Einstein asked the taxi driver who picked him up at the train station where he could obtain a drink…and then the driver handed him a bottle of booze.[382] Baltimore, at eighteen minutes and twenty-one seconds, actually paled in comparison to New Orleans, New

Famous gangster and organized crime boss Al Capone was treated for syphilis at Baltimore's Union Memorial Hospital in 1939 and gave the hospital this weeping cherry tree as a thank-you. *Michael T. Walsh.*

York, Detroit and some of the other cities yet still came in ahead of Chicago, St. Louis and Washington, D.C. Procuring liquor in Baltimore was not hard to accomplish during Prohibition.

FEDERAL VERSUS STATE ENFORCEMENT

New Year's Eve 1921 in Baltimore was hardly a dry event. The *New York Times* reported that "thousands" of bottles of whiskey, wine and beer were generously imbibed by Baltimoreans, who were celebrating the passing of yet another year. There seemed to be little or no decline in drinking in private and public establishments despite the presence of Prohibition and the potential ramifications of breaking such a law.[383]

Such a scene was seemingly not uncommon in Baltimore. By September 1922, it was acknowledged, even by federal Prohibition commissioner Roy

A. Haynes, that "Prohibition enforcement in Baltimore appeared to be a losing game."[384] Edward J. Lindholm was the acting head of Maryland's Prohibition office, and he reported to Haynes that conditions in Baltimore are "no better than…six months ago, if as good….We knock off a big still today and tomorrow there are two in its place." Homebrewing in Baltimore was virtually nonexistent because "the liquor market is too wide open" and the prices for the liquor were, for the most part, rather inexpensive.[385]

On some occasions, enforcing Prohibition meant halting the illegal manufacture and distribution of liquor even though those bootleggers often eluded arrest. In March 1922, police found a moonshine plant on East Pratt Street that was estimated to be worth at least $20,000 and could turn out 300 gallons of liquor per day.[386] It was believed to be the biggest moonshine liquor plant found in the United States since Prohibition became the law of the land. Not even two months later (May 6, 1922), a two-story brick building was raided on East Street (in East Baltimore) in which twenty-two stills, 3,500 gallons of mash and large quantities of whiskey were found. Total acquisitions from this bust were worth between $35,000 and $50,000. The building had been wholly converted to producing liquor exclusively, with all six rooms set up for distilling (seventeen stills in operation, with five new ones not yet set up). Five men, all from Brooklyn, New York, were known to be the main operators of the impromptu distillery, but the Prohibition agents were only able to capture one perpetrator.[387]

A major problem with enforcing Prohibition in Baltimore and Maryland was determining who was actually going to enforce the policy in the city and state. Maryland governor Albert C. Ritchie stated on numerous occasions that he would not collect taxes for the enforcement of Prohibition.[388] If Prohibition was to be enforced in Maryland, it would have to be enforced by federal, and not state, Prohibition agents who were part of the Prohibition Unit, which came under the U.S. Treasury Department's Bureau of Internal Revenue. The unit's agents were responsible for enforcing the National Prohibition Act, with hoped-for but often not forthcoming cooperation from local police (as well as other government entities like the U.S. Coast Guard on waterways and the Board of Customs at border entry points).[389] The main goal, according to Salisbury, Maryland native and Prohibition Bureau director Amos Walter Wright Woodcock, was to "enforce the law against the big, commercial violators."[390]

Perpetrators who were arrested for liquor violations were guaranteed their day in court. Judge John Carter Rose, a respected U.S. district judge who had been a major Progressive leader in Baltimore City, handled the most notable violations in the early days of Prohibition. Four men—William B. Fosbender, Martin Bochenski, William Berger and Thomas Malloy—who were saloonkeepers, café owners and bartenders, faced jail terms for serving drinks after January 16, 1920.[391] Judge Rose, however, did not deliver severe sentences, claiming that the wisdom of the law of Prohibition was a legislative matter and not a judicial matter. However, he did hand out jail sentences ranging from sixty days to four months.

Despite some evidence of city and state police action, federal Prohibition agents received little to no cooperation from local Baltimore police and only minimal support from the rest of Maryland's law enforcement community. Commissioner James Doran was quoted in 1928 as stating the following:

> We have no cooperation in the State of Maryland other than the sheriffs of some of the counties where they have local option laws. We thought we had secured a great deal of cooperation in the Baltimore Police Department when they agreed to protect our men from riot when they were making raids and to preserve public order. That was helpful. Before that we were thrown to the wolves over there.[392]

In 1923, nearly one thousand rioters protested and threatened bodily harm to three Prohibition agents who were attempting to disrupt the transportation of two hundred cases of real beer from a B&O Railroad car to two auto trucks. The agents had little choice, fearing personal physical harm from the gathered mob, but to let the trucks escape the site with the real beer cargo in tow. One of the trucks, with one hundred cases of beer, was eventually caught near Camden Station not much later, and the other got away.[393]

Notwithstanding the sparse evidence of Jewish opposition to (or support of) Prohibition in Maryland, there is one article from 1922 that the *Sun* did report on involving a home confrontation situated in a Jewish neighborhood in East Baltimore (140 North Exeter Street) between Prohibition agents and Mr. and Mrs. Abraham Levine. Levine was found to have had a quart of whiskey and twenty-five cases of fruit wine.[394] Levine's wife subsequently threw an alarm clock at the Prohibition agents, as neighborhood residents gathered outside the house, ready to support the Levine household if warranted.

As the decade progressed, bootleggers and rumrunners became bolder, more open and more advanced in their smuggling and evasion methods. One instance of note occurred in 1925, when four Prohibition agents were unable to keep up with two rumrunning automobiles on Washington Boulevard outside Laurel, Maryland, a notorious bootlegging route.[395] One of the rumrunning cars used a smoke screen that "enveloped the entire road and was so thick that the agents said it was impossible to see their way."[396] Both cars were able to get away. There are some documented instances where federal Prohibition agents experienced direct violence. In December 1920, federal agents and city police investigated a gunfight on Belair Road near Kingsville where a federal Prohibition agent, Lawler W. Girth of 1812 Harlem Avenue, was shot twice and an African American was mortally wounded.[397] It was believed that five African Americans were illegally transporting one pint of whiskey.

Sometimes it was the Prohibition agents who took matters into their own hands. Following a raid of an illegal still in 1924, four Prohibition agents—Wilton L. Stevens, John M. Barnes, Robert D. Ford and E. Franklin Ely—and their chauffeur, William Trabing, were charged by the State of Maryland with the murder of Harford County resident Lawrence Wenger. After causing the bootleggers to flee and unsuccessfully pursuing them, the agents returned to the still site and destroyed the materials. The agents then came upon the wounded Wenger. The agents did attempt to take the wounded man for medical treatment in Jarrettsville, Maryland (no medical treatment available), and then to Bel Air, Maryland, where Wenger was ultimately pronounced dead on arrival. The agents were charged with homicide, despite their testimonials that they were not necessarily responsible for the fatal wounds and that, in any event, this act was done under "the discharge of their official duties as prohibition agents."[398] The suspects tried to have their state murder trial remanded to federal court with an argument that as official federal Prohibition agents, they were entitled to a federal trial. In *State of Maryland v. Soper* (1926), the Supreme Court, in an opinion issued by Chief Justice (and former U.S. President) William Howard Taft, denied the petition—a writ of mandamus against District Judge Soper that would have forced the trial into federal and not state courts.

By 1927, under the leadership of Prohibition Director Lincoln C. Andrews, the Prohibition Unit had become well organized and effective. The unit was rechristened the Bureau of Prohibition and transferred from the Treasury Department to the Justice Department. There were twenty-six administrative districts with fifteen field divisions in the Bureau of Prohibition. Baltimore was one of the divisions, responsible for the geographic areas of Maryland, Virginia, West Virginia and Washington, D.C.[399]

The new Jones Act, also termed the "Five and Ten," was enacted in 1929. This law increased Prohibition punishments for violation with a five-year penitentiary sentence and a $10,000 fine. Baltimore police estimated that 5 percent of the city's 5,000 speakeasies, saloons and nightclubs (roughly 250 total) were "frightened out of business" due to this law.[400] The diplomatic liquor trade from Baltimore to D.C. (foreign embassies were not legally U.S. soil and therefore were not subject to the prohibition of alcohol) was also severely hampered by the Jones Act, as evidenced by a Washington, D.C. police raid on a truck bound for the Siam embassy that carried sixty cases of wine and liquor. The U.S. drivers were arrested for being in violation of the Jones Act, so the State Department urged foreign representatives to drive their own trucks.[401]

President Hoover planned on making Washington, D.C., one of the driest cities in the nation. To do that, he had to reshuffle some people in the Prohibition Bureau, bringing in those known for tougher enforcement and transferring others who were deemed to be too lenient or ineffective in enforcement. John F.J. Herbert, Prohibition administrator in Baltimore, whose office also included enforcement in Washington, D.C., was transferred to Helena, Montana. Thomas Elijah Stone, who had been recognized for severely curbing Detroit's liquor trade with Canada, was named as the new Prohibition administrator in Baltimore with the hope that Stone could obtain similar results in the Baltimore/Washington corridor. And there is some evidence that the reshuffling had some effect. For example, Assistant Secretary of the Navy Ernest Lee Jahncke was himself pulled over and thoroughly searched by Prohibition agents on the Baltimore Washington highway in 1930.[402] The search revealed nothing out of the ordinary, but this event perhaps does reveal that cracking down on enforcement of Prohibition was at least being taken quite seriously by some federal administrators.

The July 7, 1930 issue of *Time* reported that Amos Walter Wright Woodcock, succeeding Lincoln C. Andrews, who had completed his term, became the new director of the Prohibition Bureau. Director Woodcock was a Methodist, had served eight years as U.S. district attorney in Baltimore and lived in Salisbury.[403] With Woodcock's promotion, Baltimoreans naturally became quite interested in what he might do with his new power in their wet city. *Time* reported:

> *Baltimore citizens, wondered what Director Woodcock would do about their—and his—soaking Wet city. Speakeasies in Baltimore have run openly and in great numbers for years. Good domestic gin, most popular*

Amos Walter Wright Woodcock (*left*), Maryland native and director of the Prohibition Bureau, displaying the new insignia plate for the bureau. Also pictured are H.M. Lucious (*middle*), secretary of the Automobile Club of Maryland, and Ernest M. Smith (*right*), vice-president of the American Automobile Association. *Library of Congress, Prints and Photographs Division, Harris and Ewing Collection, LC-DIG-hec-35991.*

drink, sells for $1 per pint. Maryland moonshiners supply the city with a fair grade of whiskey while the best drug store rye (cut) can be freely obtained for $5 per pint. Good beer is to be had from Pennsylvania at 35 cents the glass. There is little or no home brewing because the liquor market is too wide open. Chesapeake Bay shipping provides wealthy Vets with expensive foreign goods. As U.S. attorney Mr. Woodcock used to leave his apartment on Charles Street every evening at 10 o'clock, walk to the corner drug store, toss down a milk shake, Coca Cola or lime phosphate. Once he set Baltimore tongues to wild wagging by escorting Mrs. Willebrandt to the opera. He failed to convict John Philip Hill, flagrantly wet onetime Congressman, for public home-brewing in Baltimore.[404]

Enforcing Baltimore's waterways was an important strategy in attempting to disrupt bootleg channels out of the Chesapeake Bay. It was usually the assignment of the U.S. Coast Guard to enforce Prohibition in ports and waterways, although the Coast Guard did receive cooperation from other federal agencies.[405] In particular, until the end of Prohibition arrived in 1933, the Baltimore/Norfolk waterway connection via the Chesapeake Bay was under constant surveillance—often by undercover agents of the Treasury and Justice Departments and the Coast Guard—for bootleg liquor shipments from one port to the other.[406]

The Chesapeake was full of rumrunners, and despite the efforts at enforcement in the area, the rumrunners were often successful in deploying and receiving their merchandise. For instance, the Baltimore Harbor patrol (the marine division of the Baltimore Police Department) searched the upper Patapsco River for five vessels shipping Scotch whiskey that originated in Nassau, Bahamas, in late August 1921. Despite coordinated efforts by Baltimore, Norfolk, Richmond and Washington Prohibition agents, the fast power boats were able to elude their potential captors by remaining in international waters for as long as possible and then slipping through the Virginia Capes in the early morning hours of August 24.[407] In response to acts such as these, it was decided in 1922 that a new "Prohibition Navy," a subset of the U.S. Coast Guard, would be formed under the direction of Lieutenant R.L. Jack. Four sub-chasers were sent to Spedden's Shipyard in the Fell's Point and Canton neighborhoods of Baltimore to be refashioned and redesigned to deter and capture rumrunning vessels. The recruiting headquarters for the "Prohibition Navy" would be based in Baltimore under Prohibition agent Elmer Kirwan.[408]

ORGANIZED CRIME

The gangster and bootlegger have been sensationalized in popular media and have come to be leading and recognizable symbols of the Roaring Twenties. Undoubtedly, organized bootlegging operations took place throughout the city and state. Yet Baltimore did not experience organized crime in the ways that cities such as Detroit and New York did. The reason for this is unclear, although it seems that the gangsters in those other cities, like New York City, were much more organized in their infrastructure and in their business methods.[409] There was also little need to hide such crime organizations if there was an already tolerated "ubiquitous presence of alcohol" on a city's streets.[410] That could have been the case in Baltimore.

Nevertheless, even though the Thompson submachine gun (aka the "Tommy gun") may not have ruled the streets of Baltimore and Maryland, there was certainly Prohibition-related crime throughout the city and state. One of the most common crimes committed during Prohibition were the repeated burglaries of still-functioning distilleries and government-bonded warehouses where alcohol was being stored for medicinal and industrial purposes. There was, for example, a failed attempt to raid the Gwynnbrook Distillery, near Owings Mills, by five men in the days immediately following enactment.[411] The five burglars shot one guard in the shoulder and gagged and bound another guard. In March 1920, $100,000 worth of Pikesville Rye Whiskey (12,500 quarts) was transported to New York before being procured by law enforcement.[412] On April 2, 1920, in Grantsville, Maryland (located in Garrett County in western Maryland), a robbery took place at the Fairchance Distillery, which was reputedly one of the most burglarized whiskey warehouses in the United States. Forty-five barrels of whiskey, estimated to be worth between $30,000 and $40,000, were removed from the warehouse.[413] As still another example, the McGinnis Distillery in Carrollton was burglarized twice during the 1920s. In November 1923, the distillery was robbed of seven barrels of liquor.[414] In January 1926, the same distillery, which by then served as a government liquor warehouse, was burglarized of nearly $100,000 worth of whiskey.[415] The robbers, led by James M. Geisey of Baltimore, were eventually indicted in April 1926.[416] The distillery, however, never opened for operation again.[417]

The forging of permits that allowed the removal of liquor from bonded warehouses for non-beverage purposes was a common bootlegger activity. In June 1920, the *New York Times* reported that there was a huge number of such forged permits discovered in New York.[418] The newspaper stated

Left: The Hotel Gunter in Frostburg, Maryland (2017 photo), a town in western Maryland that saw the bootleg trade flourish during Prohibition. *Michael T. Walsh.*

Below: The Hotel Gunter's speakeasy, a small but effective room for evading enforcement, drinking alcohol and betting on roosters during the 1920s. *Michael T. Walsh.*

The Owl Bar and its blinking-eyes owl perched high above the bar, located in Baltimore's Belvedere Hotel at 1 East Chase Street. *Michael T. Walsh.*

that although no forgeries had yet been uncovered, "similar illegal practices have been discovered in Maryland," including whiskey permits whose figures had been raised.[419] In an attempt to enforce the rule, all permits were then ordered to be returned before any of the whiskey would be delivered. However, it is not surprising that, not many months later, it was reported that forged permits had become a problem in Baltimore and Maryland. On January 8, 1921, Prohibition agents and Baltimore City detectives arrested eight men who possessed whiskey that was valued at about $100,000. This was a major operation since it was believed that these arrests would stop a "plot to get whisky from bonded warehouses through fraudulent withdrawal permits" that could then be transported to large cities up and down the East Coast.[420] In October 1921, Baltimorean Samuel Albrecht was arrested in New York in the reception room of Prohibition Enforcement Director E.C. Yellowley's office on a bribery charge ($200 offered to Yellowley's chief assistant for permission to inspect Yellowley's files regarding whiskey withdrawal permits). Apprehending Albrecht was deemed to be a major coup in suspending the operations of a "gang of wealthy bootleggers."[421]

The emergence of speakeasies within the city and the counties of Maryland provides further evidence that illegal activity was occurring. In Frostburg, Maryland, a popular speakeasy was established in the bowels of the Gunter Hotel. The entrance to the speakeasy was located close to the train tracks that delivered coal for the hotel's furnace. Beneath the coal, illicit liquor was transported to the speakeasy, which functioned as a drinking establishment and a place to wage bets on cock fights. It is said that Frostburg's German Arion Band "would play on the balcony of the hotel while booze was hustled out the back" to distract any would-be enforcement officials from halting the smuggling.[422] Gunter Hotel's speakeasy and cockfighting pit remains amazingly preserved and on display at the hotel to this day; it is a must-see if you visit Frostburg.[423]

Baltimore City had numerous speakeasies in its city limits. The most well-known speakeasy is today known as the Owl Bar, located in the Belvedere Hotel. It is believed that if the eyes of the owls (one is still perched above the bar to this day) were blinking, then liquor was available and no Prohibition agents were around to bust up the gathering.[424] If the eyes did not blink, "'the wise old owl' sat on his barstool, spoke less and heard more."[425] This was a signal to the patrons to be on their best behavior and speak nothing of alcohol availability. Another late-era speakeasy was located in the Lord Baltimore Hotel, which opened in 1928. The location of this speakeasy was just recently rediscovered behind a wall in the hotel's restaurant during renovations of the hotel in 2016 after it went "missing" for decades.[426] It now operates as a cocktail bar once again, appropriately branded as the LB Speakeasy.

A BALTIMORE "CRIME WAVE"?

In *Chesapeake Rum Runners of the Roaring Twenties*, historian Eric Mills stated that a crime wave "engulfed" the Chesapeake region soon after the enactment of Prohibition in 1920.[427] Mills's assessment echoes the traditional argument that the enactment of Prohibition led to a great increase of crime in America throughout the 1920s. However, some prominent academic histories have deviated from this traditional evaluation. Historian John C. Burnham, for example, has noted:

> *During the 1920's there was almost universal public belief that a "crime wave" existed in the United States. In spite of the literary output on the*

subject, dealing largely with a local situation in Chicago, there is no firm evidence of this supposed upsurge in lawlessness....The crime wave, in other words, was the invention of enterprising journalists feeding on some sensational crimes and situations and catering to a public to whom the newly discovered "racketeer" was a covert folk hero.[428]

In Baltimore police commissioner Charles D. Gaither's 1932 annual report to Governor Ritchie, the commissioner stated that "I am confident that organized crime does not exist in this City and experience has proven that as a result of one arrest involving burglary or robbery, several other complaints are cleared by the defendant confessing to crimes previously reported."[429] A statement like this from someone who was privy to all information concerning crime in the city obviously is at odds with any argument that organized crime was important in Baltimore during Prohibition, and there is no evidence that he was being anything but frank (although as commissioner, he surely was biased in his assessment as well).

The idea that Prohibition resulted in a decade-long "crime wave" in Baltimore seems mistaken. While there is anecdotal evidence that reveals that criminal activity occurred as a direct result of Prohibition, there is other evidence that reveals that a "crime wave" might not have taken place in Baltimore during this era. Indeed, available statistical data does not point to a significant increase in crime in Baltimore City due to Prohibition.

Examining the *Reports of the Police Commissioner for the City of Baltimore* during the years of Prohibition discloses the types and totals of arrests made in Baltimore City. The two arrest records that can be directly attributed to Prohibition laws are those of Prohibition law violations and drunkenness. The commissioner never explicitly stated that Prohibition was directly responsible for the climbing homicide rate or the increase of automobile violations. In fact, although TABLE 7 shows an increase in Baltimore's arrest rate for drinking and driving in the early 1920s, it was rather small in comparison to other major cities, including its direct southern neighbor Washington, D.C.[430]

TABLE 8 shows the arrest records in Baltimore between 1917 and 1934.[431] Total crime and the number of arrests did increase during the 1920s. The total number of arrests actually *tripled* between the early 1920s and the early 1930s. However, the assumption that Prohibition and the consumption of alcohol were accountable for the increase in crime is an incorrect analysis. Even the total number of arrests for 1918, prior to Prohibition, was higher than the total number of arrests in 1922—two years after Prohibition was

A 1925 photo depicts residents of Bay Ridge, near Annapolis, possibly enjoying some illicit liquor during a recreational drive. *Collection of the Maryland State Archives (MSA-SC 2140-1-181).*

implemented. This might signify that a slowly rising trend in crime was occurring even prior to Prohibition.[432]

Statistics for Prohibition law violations were first officially recorded for the year 1921. Although Prohibition law violations increased in the first three years, TABLE 8 shows that those violations accounted on average for less than 1 percent (0.93 percent) of the total arrests made in Baltimore from 1921 through 1923. Although the total number of arrests for violating the Prohibition law quadrupled from 1921 through 1932 (as the total number of arrests roughly doubled), the violations during the Prohibition period account for less than 1 percent (0.92 percent) of the total arrests made. The percentage of arrests for violating the Prohibition law remained fairly constant throughout the 1920s, never exceeding 1.20 percent of all arrests made in Baltimore. This result nearly matches the average of the 1921–23 period, showing a remarkable consistency in the number of violations and arrests in Baltimore.

It is worth noting that the arrests for drunkenness on the whole decreased from a high of 7,552 in 1918 to 1,785 in 1920. By 1922, the arrests for drunkenness (4,955) had risen to almost 5,000, which nearly equaled drunkenness arrests for 1917 (5,129). The percentage of arrests made for drunkenness during Prohibition never equaled the percentage high of 12.2 percent that was recorded in 1918, a full two years before the full implementation of Prohibition. Perhaps the enforcement of Prohibition did not cause a crime epidemic. Or perhaps without Prohibition and the threat of arrest, the percentage of arrests for drunkenness during the 1920s may have continued to steadily rise. One can only speculate.

The percentage of arrests made related to drunkenness and/or Prohibition laws from 1917 through 1925 is a bit inconsistent, but for the most part, it does show a gradual downward trend from a high of 12.2 percent in 1918 to 7.2 percent in 1925. The combined percentage actually continued to decrease or at least remain constant throughout the rest of the decade and into the early 1930s. The percentage of arrests never exceeded the 1926 high of 6.2 percent (and therefore the percentage of arrests also never increased past the higher percentages from the years 1917–25), generally decreasing as the years progressed.

On average, then, it seems that as total arrests and total residents increased, only a small percentage of the crime had much to do with Prohibition and only a small percentage of the population was arrested for Prohibition-related crime. This finding might provide further evidence for the effectiveness of Prohibition and its enforcement in the city, no matter how wet Baltimore was. The evidence suggests that the percentage of Baltimore's population arrested for Prohibition-related crime remained fairly proportional to the total arrest percentage, despite the population growth. Thus, it can be argued with these records that a greater number of people in the city did not create more crime related to and caused by Prohibition.

These statistical findings seem to have some historical corroboration as well. During the Senate hearings on the national Prohibition law in 1926, Senator William Cabell Bruce of Maryland offered remarkable statistics showing that Baltimore's arrests for drunkenness violations from 1920 to 1925 (28,149 arrests) were lower than average when compared to other major U.S. cities. Senator Bruce stated the following in his address to the Subcommittee of the Committee of the Judiciary that not only reveals Baltimore's seeming indifference and "hostility" toward Prohibition but also may vouch for the effectiveness of Prohibition in curtailing the public drunkenness that was once on display at Baltimore's saloons.

The claim has been made that this record of arrests for drunkenness is misleading, because since the enactment of the Volstead Act police officers are quicker to arrest persons under the influence of liquor than they were before that time. This is certainly not so in Baltimore, the city with which I am most familiar, because the standing instructions of our police commissioner as to the degree of intoxication that justifies arrest are the same as those that obtained before the passage of the Volstead Act, and there is every reason, besides, to believe that Baltimore city policemen share the hostility to Prohibition which is entertained by the great majority of the people of Baltimore. Even if different conditions exist in other cities, it should be borne in mind that, at the present time, drunkenness is not so visible to the policeman, however alert to arrest, as it was when drink addicts did not get drunk on bootleg liquor or home brew in the home, but on liquor at the corner saloon.[433]

One must, of course, state the possibility that some cities, like Baltimore and New York, may have been more lenient due to their wet proclivity (i.e., those municipalities did not report all of their arrests for drunkenness and may not have even made an arrest at all), and some cities may have been stricter in enforcement and tabulating arrests for drunkenness. Of course, since Baltimore was indeed so wet, one must also consider the possibility that lax enforcement might have caused some of the arrest figures to be less than actual.

These findings do not signify that Baltimore was clear of any criminal activity, as there is ample evidence that assuredly states otherwise. These findings might never be totally conclusive in revealing what actually happened during that period of time. But the data does suggest that the "crime wave" that was allegedly caused by Prohibition never quite crashed over Baltimore.

Chapter 6

THE POLITICS OF PROHIBITION

*Give the settlement of local problems back to the localities concerned, and our
history of previous success will continue.*
—U.S. Senator Millard E. Tydings (D) of Maryland[434]

The sentiment provided by Senator Tydings captures the general attitude toward national Prohibition from many of Baltimore's and Maryland's major leaders. Of all the issues and concerns that were directly and indirectly related to Prohibition, the largest predicament with the policy in Maryland was probably the persistent debate over determining and then establishing the proper allocation of local, state and federal power. A *TIME* magazine article from 1930 noted that "persons rather than policies define the degrees of Wetness."[435] No matter what the policy may have stated, it was the people and the leaders they followed who ultimately determined the effectiveness of Prohibition. And in Maryland, some of the leaders and many voters were gloriously wet.

GOVERNOR ALBERT C. RITCHIE (D)

Governor Albert C. Ritchie, a Democrat, was a graduate of University of Maryland Law School who then entered public service in Baltimore working in the city solicitor's office and as part of the Public Service Commission. He

Maryland governor Albert C. Ritchie (D). *Library of Congress, Prints and Photographs Division, Bain Collection, LC-DIG-ggbain-29462.*

rose to state prominence when he became attorney general in 1915. In 1919, Ritchie ran in the state's gubernatorial race against Republican Harry W. Nice and won by a margin of just 165 votes.[436] His 1919 victory became his first of four elections as Maryland's governor.

Ritchie took the oath of office as governor of Maryland just as national Prohibition was implemented in January 1920. Prohibition was, not surprisingly, an issue in the 1919 gubernatorial election. It was during this campaign that Ritchie inextricably linked his name to the fight against Prohibition based on a states' rights argument and a belief that dual federalism was the traditional and correct structure for governance. He stated on numerous occasions that Prohibition would only be enforced in Maryland if federal forces and Prohibition Unit agents intervened.[437] Ritchie argued that the problem with Prohibition was a problem of jurisdiction—the federal and state governments should operate in separate spheres regarding the issue of Prohibition.[438]

Ritchie's words and actions after his narrow victory in 1919, particularly regarding Prohibition, were those of a man who did not lack political confidence. And Prohibition was the issue that he really made into his own personal crusade, one that would garner much public support among eligible Baltimore and Maryland voters. As early as 1920, Ritchie exhibited public opposition to Prohibition in the state legislature (urging to let Maryland farmers produce 3.5 percent cider) and at the National Democratic Convention (where he wanted a wet national platform for the Democrats).[439] Ritchie did not fight the ideal of temperance, however; he fought Prohibition because he believed it to be a violation of states' rights and an infringement on personal liberties.[440]

This principled and unwavering states' rights philosophy seemed to endear him not only to wets in Maryland but also to others in America. In December 1922, at the Fourteenth Annual Conference of Governors, Ritchie and eighteen other state governors were invited to a luncheon to discuss the Eighteenth Amendment with President Warren G. Harding. The

New York Times noted that Ritchie was the "only one…who came out flatly with the statement that the majority of his constituents did not believe that the Volstead could be enforced."[441] Ritchie argued that Marylanders were "effectively solving the temperance question by local option in the various units of the State…under that method when the people of a community wanted prohibition they actually got it."[442] Ritchie's public proclamations at this meeting led historian William Bowen to conclude that "Ritchie's position was Maryland's, and Maryland's becoming that of most of the nation."[443]

However, it was a speech given by Governor Ritchie at the Institute of Public Affairs at the University of Virginia on August 14, 1929, that was the most straightforward attack on national Prohibition and provides the best example of Ritchie's views on prohibition and states' rights:

> *National Prohibition is not a success and the sooner we admit it the sooner we shall find a way to do something constructive.…Maryland does not construe it. Because we do not, we are accused by militant drys of treason, sedition, secession, nullification, and every other high crime and misdemeanor in the catalogue of prohibition abuse.…All this is sheer nonsense. The people of Maryland are as patriotic, as law-abiding and as law-respecting as the people of any other State.*[444]

On November 23, 1933, just weeks before repeal, Governor Ritchie called the General Assembly into special session to discuss the regulation and control of alcohol in the state of Maryland. Ritchie wanted to "devise a method of liquor control which will do away with the evils National Prohibition brought about without reestablishing the evils which brought about National Prohibition."[445] Ritchie favored local option, which was "in accord with Maryland traditions and practices," to determine if regions in the state wanted to be dry or wet.[446] He also recognized that hard liquor, which was more potent than beer, posed more of a potential problem to society. Because of this, he favored higher restrictions on the retail of liquor than on beer by requiring a higher license fee and "stricter conditions" for liquor than on a license for beer.[447] Ritchie undoubtedly wanted alcohol in the state. But he also wanted the ability for the state, and *not* the federal government, to control liquor within Maryland's boundaries. Even in victory, Ritchie remained steadfast in his states' rights principles.

U.S. SENATOR WILLIAM CABELL BRUCE (D)

William Cabell Bruce, a Democrat, served as a Maryland senator from 1923 to 1929.[448] During his one term as senator, Bruce earned the reputation as an anti-prohibitionist and states' rights advocate. An example of Senator Bruce's quick wit and sharp criticism occurred when Alabama senator James Thomas Heflin (D) stated to his Senate colleagues that "there are so few wet advocates in the Senate they could be put inside a taxicab." Senator Bruce quickly fired back with a stinging rebuke that "[well], the number of senators who decline a drink when it is offered to them could be put into a smaller cubic content than a taxicab."[449]

Maryland senator William Cabell Bruce (D). *Library of Congress, Prints and Photographs Division, Bain Collection, LC-DIG-ggbain-35131.*

Senator Bruce advocated the position held by Governor Ritchie that the states—not the federal government—should be allowed to control and enforce liquor and alcohol traffic. During the national Prohibition law hearings in 1926, Bruce stated that the federal government's role in enforcing Prohibition had been "pertinaciously" carried out as a policy, ignorant and "obnoxious" to the popular opinion of Prohibition.[450]

Bruce defended his belief that local option was the only way to control liquor in America. His preferred model for liquor control was termed the Quebec Plan, which had been established in Quebec, Canada, in 1921 and had favored the sales of wine and beer in local stores over hard liquor and spirits.[451] This Quebec Plan or a similar plan was favored by the Local Self Government League of Baltimore as well. In 1931, the league printed a pamphlet that proudly declared that it was against "Volsteadism."[452] The plan preserved local option but had a provincial liquor commission that would conduct the liquor trade through government-run dispensaries to benefit the government, through revenues gained by sales and taxes on the alcohol.[453] Senator Bruce reported that the plan had been a success, for the promotion of wine over spirits had led to a decrease in drunkenness and had also had a financial sales increase as well.[454]

Senator Bruce's suggestions in 1926 mostly fell on deaf ears or were severely criticized by others in the government. One such critic was Senator Hugo L. Black (D) of Alabama, who proved to be a nemesis of Senator Bruce's in regards to Prohibition. Black made a scathing rebuke of Bruce's views in May 1928 in the *Congressional Record*. Black, a self-proclaimed and proud southern prohibitionist, stated:

> It is easy for the Senator…to claim they know more about what happens in West Virginia than do the citizens and the duly constituted legal authorities of that State. It is easy to loudly assert the idea of state rights and then attempt to govern the country precincts of West Virginia from Baltimore or New York. All you have to do is take a trip over into the State of Maryland. There you find a system of lawlessness which is unparalleled and unprecedented anywhere in America except the State of New York. Why is that? Because of the fact that sentiments like those we have heard expressed here from day to day and from week to week have filled the people of that State with the belief that displeased individuals are bigger than the law.…Does America want a country of law or does it want a country of anarchy? If it wants anarchy, listen to the preachments of the men who proclaim the doctrine of the Sen. from Maryland, the Governor of Maryland, and the various other people whose doctrines would trample underfoot the sacred principles of American liberty, American hope, and American constitutional government.[455]

Senator Bruce faced a highly regarded candidate in his 1928 quest for reelection: Republican Phillips Lee Goldsborough, a Baltimore banker and a popular former governor of Maryland from 1912 to 1916.[456] In June 1928, the *Morning Sun* projected that in order for Bruce to win reelection, he would need to receive a majority of between twenty to twenty-five thousand votes in Baltimore City. Bruce used his anti-Prohibition stance as one of his primary means for attracting potential voters, not unlike Democratic presidential candidate Alfred E. Smith. Bruce felt that Prohibition was the main issue in 1928:

> Prohibition will be the leading, if not the only real issue of the campaign, at least, it will be the pivotal issue.…I expect many dry Democrats to vote for Hoover, but I expect myriads of Republicans favoring a change in the Prohibition law to flock to Smith's standard.…The majority of Maryland

voters of both parties will heartily approve the stand of Governor Smith for dry law modification.[457]

Goldsborough was generally thought to be a dry (he lived in heavily dry Dorchester County and was born in Princess Anne, Maryland, in Somerset County) but was politically savvy in not publicly proclaiming just how dry or wet he actually was, enabling him to not alienate either dry or wet supporters. Goldsborough's views on Prohibition were much more guarded than Bruce's, for there was "no record of his ever having made a definite statement to the degree of his dryness."[458]

Goldsborough received 54.1 percent (256,224) of the vote to Bruce's 45.2 percent (214,447).[459] Bruce carried wet Baltimore City by only 3,412 votes (50.3 percent), well short of what he needed to win by in the city, a result that was somewhat surprising to both candidates.[460] Accounts of the election results do not attribute the issue of Prohibition and the candidates' views on the policy to the reason why Bruce did not receive a more substantial portion of the popular vote in wet Baltimore. One must assume that other issues may have determined the outcome. The *New York Times* did report that "Senator Bruce's independence has not pleased many Democrats and his assaults upon prohibition are said to have injured his chances in dry Democratic rural sections of the State."[461] George W. Crabbe, superintendent of the Maryland Anti-Saloon League, commented that the wetness of Bruce and what Crabbe perceived as growing unpopularity of Governor Ritchie were reasons for Bruce's loss to Goldsborough, claiming that Bruce lost the Democrat vote due to people having grown "tired of Ritchie's kind of politics."[462] Crabbe then iterated that "a vote for Goldsborough is a vote for State enforcement act for Maryland."[463]

Bruce returned to practicing law in Baltimore and was not in public office when Prohibition came to an end in 1933.[464] Even after leaving the Senate, however, Bruce tried repeatedly to push for modification of the Volstead Act. He even appealed to the Association Against the Prohibition Amendment (AAPA) in 1930 to construct a national wet convention that would expressly deal with drafting such a modification or reform. Bruce was more than happy to offer his opinion on the prospects of repeal on September 13, 1933, the day after Maryland's delegates were elected to the state convention to ratify the Twenty-First Amendment. Mr. Bruce stated that he thought the elections were "one of the most remarkable illustrations of popular government at its best."[465] He urged the victors to hold no bitterness toward prohibitionists; the fight had been won, and there was no need to gloat.[466]

U.S. Representative John Philip Hill (R)

John Philip Hill was one of the more colorful characters in the story of Prohibition in Baltimore. Hill was a Maryland native and Baltimore lawyer who served in several public offices, including an unsuccessful campaign for the mayor of Baltimore in 1915.[467] After returning home from fighting in World War I, Hill joined the Republican Party and was elected in 1920 to the U.S. House of Representatives (Maryland, Third District), even though this district was largely a Democratic stronghold.[468] In 1922, the *Evening Sun* polled 4,320 returning servicemen to see if they would hypothetically favor a tax on beer and light wines to help pay for the soldiers' bonus, if such sales of alcohol were still allowed.[469] About 99 percent of the soldiers said yes to this poll question.[470] Soon after this *Sun* poll, Hill began to see that favoring and "whooping for beer was good politics" in the city and state.[471] *Time* magazine noted, "John Philip loves publicity....He lives by headlines. If newspapers were abolished, he would curl up and die."[472]

Hill thought that the Volstead Act was unfair to those who lived in the city, citing specifically that the act permitted farmers to make wine and cider not exceeding 0.5 percent.[473] So Hill decided to rename his house Franklin Farms (since it was located at 3 West Franklin Street) and proceeded to plant apple saplings and grapevines in his backyard.[474] He would then press the fruit and store it, knowing all too well that the product would ferment. He claimed that only the actual cider and wine, and not his own person, were breaking the Prohibition law.[475]

Hill's interest in the *Evening Sun* poll led him to introduce a bill in the House that proposed to pay a soldiers' bonus from the tax revenues of light wine and beers. This bill was also backed and fully supported by a Baltimore City Council resolution.[476] For Hill, this would prove to be a highly logical resolution to two problems. He argued that the bonuses could be paid off (net about $2.5 billion) to the soldiers within five years if the Volstead Act were modified to allow for light beer and wine. However, the bill was never passed. Hill was also one of the earliest advocates to urge that Prohibition enforcement be moved from the Treasury Department to the Department of Justice.[477] This reorganization eventually occurred—nearly ten years after he first advocated for it.

In September 1924, Representative Hill invited Prohibition agents and chemists, particularly Mr. H.G. Byers, head chemist of the Prohibition Unit, to his homestead to test the grape juice/wine he was making (the jar that contained the New York grapes produced more alcohol by volume, 12.64

Maryland representatives John Philip Hill (R) and John C. Linthicum (D) in 1927. The title of this photo indicates that Hill's aim is "to keep the country wet." *Library of Congress, Prints and Photographs Division, National Photo Company Collection, LC-USZ62-111366.*

percent, than the two jars of Maryland's Anne Arundel County grapes—11.8 percent ABV and 8.44 percent ABV, respectively).[478] Despite this public exhibit, Hill was initially only given a temporary injunction in which a padlock was placed on the door to the winemaking cellar.[479] However, Hill was soon arrested by federal agents and tried in a U.S. District Court. The jury found that his drink was not intoxicating, even though the alcoholic content was over 12 percent. This finding by the jury enabled Hill to be released.[480]

Several weeks later, Hill was indicted for making and possessing 2.75 percent cider at his home residence. After previously trying and failing in 1923 to get a ruling on what the maximum percentage of alcohol was allowable by the Volstead Act, Hill succeeded on this occasion. His goal was to try to provide a true definition of what was intoxicating. Hill was acquitted on the six counts of illegal manufacture and possession and for public nuisance, but the decision did not establish a definition of what an intoxicating beverage was in the Volstead Act, as Hill had hoped.[481] Federal District Court judge Morris A. Soper (of Baltimore, Maryland) interpreted the Volstead Act to mean that the home brewer of cider and juices was exempt from the 0.5 percent definition of intoxicating due to it being in a private residence as opposed to a public establishment."[482]

After a failed run at a Senate seat in 1926 and unsuccessful attempt to return to the House in 1928, Hill retired from public office.[483] On March 23, 1933, the *Evening Sun* contained numerous articles about the not-too-distant return of beer to Maryland. Hill declared in one article that he wanted beer to be sold as freely as ginger ale, sarsaparilla and milk.[484] In October 1933, when the State of Maryland formally ratified the Twenty-First Amendment, Hill had the opportunity to act as temporary chairman of the twenty-four-delegate group that voted for repeal. Hill was formally attired in what he called his "pallbearer costume" and said that "for years I have waited to be the pallbearer at the funeral of prohibition and now the opportunity has arrived."[485] He recognized the historical significance of repealing a constitutional amendment and hailed the ratification of the Twenty-First Amendment as a return of "original freedom" to the Constitution.[486]

BALTIMORE MAYOR HOWARD W. JACKSON (D)

Howard W. Jackson (D) served four terms as mayor of Baltimore. His first term was from 1923 through 1927, and his subsequent terms began in 1931 and lasted until 1943. Jackson's stand against Prohibition was based on the idea of the need for local self-rule and the feeling that dual federalism should act as a constraint on federal power. It was also well known that Jackson not only supported Ritchie's views on Prohibition but that he also partook freely of alcoholic drinks.[487] He may have been among the wettest of the wet in Baltimore at one point in the 1920s. Although Mayor Jackson became a recovering alcoholic by 1933, ending years of excessive drinking,

Harris and Ewing's 1935 photograph of two famous wets: Baltimore mayor Howard W. Jackson (D), *left*, and New York City mayor Fiorello La Guardia (R). *Library of Congress, Prints and Photographs Division, Harris and Ewing Collection, LC-DIG-hec-39632.*

terminating his personal drinking habits did not cause him to abandon his principles and belief in federalism.

Mayor Jackson played a role in helping to formulate the Democrats' repeal/modification plank for the Democratic Convention in 1932.[488] In fact, his convention hotel room was used for meetings and in efforts to formulate a consistent Prohibition platform to incorporate into the plank. When beer returned to Baltimore in April 1933, Mayor Jackson, who by then was a recovering alcoholic, did attempt to put local limits on beer distribution. Jackson wanted beer sold only from city-licensed dispensaries (at a charge of $250 per license); however, the brewing and hospitality industries convinced Jackson to drop the idea of city-run dispensaries, and he dropped the license fee to only $50.[489] Jackson's initial preference for city dispensaries would have still been in accordance with his belief in local rule. Although his initial calls for dispensaries and higher licensing fees were not implemented, what was implemented may have been more in accordance with what the public actually wanted. In that regard, his acquiescence to his constituents (and the lobbyists) was still in keeping with his personal and governing principles of local self-rule.

INTEREST GROUPS

In Maryland, the ASL experienced quantifiable success in the early twentieth century. William H. Anderson served as the state superintendent of the ASL in Maryland for seven years (1906–13) before assuming the same position for the ASL in New York. Under Anderson's control in Maryland, the ASL did have some success, despite the failure to have a statewide bill passed. The closing of saloons in Baltimore was at least partly due to the efforts of Anderson and the ASL. The number of saloons in Baltimore decreased from roughly 2,411 to 1,403 during Anderson's tenure, and the average price for a saloon license skyrocketed from $250 to $1,000.[490] The ASL was able to influence policy and decisions even in a city and state as wet as Baltimore and Maryland during this time before national Prohibition. As the years progressed under Prohibition, the ASL's influence and its supporters within Maryland's political structure receded, prompting the ASL in Maryland to seek aid from the national ASL organization and the federal government in hopes of implementing its dry visions.

Because of their wet propensity, some of Maryland's leaders listened to other interest groups they felt represented the best interests of the state. One such group was the Association Against the Prohibition Amendment (AAPA). Captain William H. Stayton, president of the Baltimore Steamship Company (a profitable shipping business in Baltimore), organized the AAPA sometime in 1918 by sending out a "solicitation letter to the six hundred men in his address book."[491] Stayton initially tried to keep names of members private due to his "innate timidity" and his own "perception of upper-class manners."[492] When the membership roll was eventually made public, the AAPA's membership included some of the wealthiest men in America, including luminaries such as Kermit Roosevelt, Vincent Astor and even John Philip Sousa.[493]

By December 1920, Stayton had enrolled thirty thousand people, mainly on the East Coast. More than one thousand of its members were Baltimoreans, and the *Evening Sun* reported that they included Marylanders of high social standing.[494] Prominent Baltimore businessmen, lawyers and physicians—including Frank A. Furst (chairman of the board of the Arundel Corporation), Dr. Alan C. Woods (of Johns Hopkins) and Alfred R. Riggs (of Riggs-Linthicum Company)—were early members of the AAPA.[495] By the early 1930s, the AAPA consisted of forty-eight state leagues, with local chapters governed throughout by superintendents, secretaries and education directors. For nine years, the main office of the AAPA was located in Baltimore.

Between 1919 and 1928, the AAPA spent upward of $60 million nationwide in order to influence elections and legislation.[496] In 1922, Captain Stayton even threatened the formation of a third party, its candidates sanctioned by the AAPA, if the Democrats and Republicans failed to include a wet plank in the 1924 election.[497] Stayton reiterated his aims together with two other objectives just five days later during a speech in Baltimore when he called for a revolt of the city voters against rural voters and for complete organization of voters in "pivotal" cities in states such as New York, Maryland, Massachusetts, Illinois and New Jersey.[498]

In fact, there was much talk and controversy about who and what the AAPA legally or illegally funded. In a letter to *Time* magazine, Governor Ritchie responded to an article that stated that the AAPA financed wet speakers like himself. Ritchie did not like the implication that he received direct funding and finances from the AAPA, and he resolutely denied having ever received any such funds for speeches or traveling purposes.[499] Ritchie was politically astute enough to avoid any official connection that might cost him an election victory, as he was likely cognizant of the mediocre results of past AAPA endorsements in previous elections. Nevertheless, the AAPA did support the victorious campaign of Representative John Charles Linthicum (D) of Maryland, a well-known wet and avid supporter of the AAPA whose family also shared a business with AAPA member Alfred C. Riggs.[500]

Despite the increased influence and power of the AAPA, it was really the Great Depression that provided the AAPA with the best opportunity of achieving its repeal aims. The AAPA repeatedly claimed that a repeal of Prohibition could mean a potential increase in federal tax revenues from alcohol sales, which celebrated businessman Pierre du Pont had thought might be in the neighborhood of $2 billion.[501] The AAPA argued that liquor sales and the taxes from those liquor sales might help the federal government stimulate the economy. Of course, there was also the overwhelming sentiment among the rich and powerful in the AAPA that repeal of Prohibition and a return to the levying of alcohol taxes might also lead to their desired demise of the federal income tax (which had been advocated in 1913 by the drys as a means to offset the loss of tax revenue from alcohol sales).[502] Unfortunately for those who advocated this position, the death of Prohibition did not precipitate the death of the income tax.

DID PROHIBITION AFFECT MAJOR ELECTION OUTCOMES?

Analyzing elections and their outcomes has seemingly become a pastime in modern America. Thus, reviewing select elections from the Prohibition period can be a fun exercise in determining the impact an election might have had on Prohibition. And it also provides a measure of public opinion on the Eighteenth Amendment itself at certain points in time.

The presidential elections of 1928 and 1932 featured Prohibition as one of the most prominent issues on the campaign trail. Both the 1928 and, to a lesser extent, the 1932 presidential elections provided a highly visible public forum between the wets and drys and their vision on the function of Prohibition in America. An argument can be made that in elections in Maryland, Prohibition played an important role in people's lives and shaped their perspectives and, perhaps, their voting preferences as well.

The 1928 Presidential Election

There will be many analyses of the elections; and historians will no doubt find a place for the many results which now appear so confusing.
—*Senator William Cabell Bruce (D) of Maryland*[503]

The degree to which Prohibition played a major role in the 1928 presidential election between the Protestant Republican Herbert Hoover and the Catholic Democratic Party nominee Alfred Smith continues to be debated among scholars. Certainly, Prohibition "stimulated more interest than any other campaign issue" in 1928.[504] Newspapers like the *Sun* kept Prohibition as a front-and-center issue in the months leading up to Election Day, by roundly criticizing Hoover for his belief that Prohibition was a "noble experiment" and praising Smith for his stance against the present law and his advocacy for its modification.[505]

As late as September 1928, just two months before the election, the issue of Prohibition in Baltimore seemed to be "the primary focus of the campaign."[506] Hoover and the Republicans tended to support enforcement of Prohibition, whereas Smith was an ardent wet who supported modification, even as some members of his Democratic Party greatly opposed his wet views. One week before the election, Al Smith arrived in Baltimore and delivered a speech before fourteen thousand people at the Fifth Regiment Armory. Smith, in what was described by Baltimore residents as the largest demonstration since Armistice Day, devoted part of his speech to lambasting both the Anti-Saloon League and the Ku Klux Klan.[507] Smith's rants against these organizations show how Smith battled prohibitionists as well as the anti-Catholic sentiment that groups like the KKK advocated. In Baltimore, home of many wets and many Catholics, such speech generated great publicity and high praise from its residents and leaders in attendance.[508] His attempt at listing both the ASL and the Klan as "allies of Republicans" might have been a last-ditch effort for Democratic votes, hoping to recoup some dry members of his own party. Prohibition and religion seemed to be the issues that garnered the most headlines going into Election Day.[509]

Nevertheless, on November 6, 1928, Americans went to the polls and voted for Hoover, who received 58.2 of the popular vote and 444 Electoral College votes; Smith's popular vote was 40.8, and he received just 87 Electoral College votes.[510] Marylanders overwhelmingly voted for Hoover, as the Republican won 57 percent of the popular vote in Maryland. The similar percentages suggest that Maryland's voters were not dissimilar from the voters in the other states and that Hoover's campaign messages had been embraced by the state. Smith fared only slightly better with voters in Maryland (42.3 percent) than nationally (40.8 percent). Hoover carried all but two counties, including a victory in the wet, heavily Catholic and immigrant-populated Baltimore City. Smith only won the two Maryland counties, winning handedly in St. Mary's County—perhaps aided by the high percentage, 77 percent, of Catholic voters[511]—and barely edging Hoover (by 34 votes) in Queen Anne's County.

The overall vote in Baltimore was indeed closer than in other areas of the state, as Hoover defeated Smith by 9,076 votes (+3.34 percent). Smith only fared better in Maryland in Howard County (losing 208 votes or -3.2 percent) and the two counties he won. Still, Smith, a Democrat, a wet and a Catholic, failed to defeat Hoover in a city that was wet with a substantial Catholic population (~38 percent).[512] Smith's crushing defeats in Baltimore County (39.6 percent), Harford County (35.1 percent) and Anne Arundel County (38.2 percent)—counties that distance-wise were not far from wet Baltimore City—may suggest that Prohibition, despite its inclusion in many of the candidates' public speeches and in the daily newspaper headlines, was not the prominent issue that determined the outcome of the election of 1928 in Maryland.

This resounding victory by Hoover has led historians and scholars to question the magnitude and impact of Prohibition on the election outcome. Allan Lichtman pointed out that historians will often overstate or understate the importance of Prohibition, often depending on their perspective and methods (traditional versus quantitative).[513] Lichtman acknowledged that Prohibition played at least a small role in voting behavior in 1928; however, the election was a "phony referendum" on Prohibition, with Hoover carrying almost every state in the Union, including states that had rejected Prohibition in statewide referenda.[514] Hoover's win was not, therefore, a public ratification of his party's dry platform. Instead, Lichtman ascertained that a cluster of ethno-cultural issues—but religion in particular—was the biggest determinant of voting behavior in the 1928 election.[515]

Shannon Lee Parsley's thesis on Baltimore during the 1928 election confirms that the distribution of the vote in Baltimore was shaped largely by ethno-cultural issues, as opposed to Prohibition or class divisions.[516] Voting behavior in Baltimore was influenced more by religion—specifically votes for and against Smith's Catholicism—than by the Prohibition issue. Although Smith polled 48.3 percent in wet Baltimore City, anti-Catholic sentiment, even in a city whose Catholic population was relatively high, seemed to have hindered Smith, suggesting that religion may have played a bigger role than Prohibition in voter preferences. Prohibition, it seems, was important to American and Baltimore voters in 1928; however, other issues such as anti-Catholic sentiment, or a cluster of entangling ethno-cultural issues, seemed to have been of more significance than *just* the issue of Prohibition.

The 1930 Congressional Election

The Congressional election of 1930 was also thought to have been greatly affected by the issue of Prohibition. An *Evening Sun* article quoted Walter H. Buck, chairman of the Maryland division of the AAPA in 1930, as stating that "certainly, the question of prohibition was the major issue in the contest."[517] Nationally, anti-prohibitionists felt this election reflected "a changing public sentiment toward Prohibition."[518] And in Maryland, Prohibition may have been an even more pivotal issue, since Governor Ritchie was running for reelection and his stance on Prohibition was well known to voters. Ritchie won the election decidedly by more than sixty-six thousand votes. Although Prohibition may have played some important role in voter turnout and may have even affected the division of the vote, the 1930 election was also not a referendum on Prohibition. The vote swing in the United States and in Maryland toward the Democrats that occurred in 1930 was primarily due to the Great Depression and to public dissatisfaction with the national Republican Party and Herbert Hoover. The wets, mostly Democrats, who did win seats in Congress primarily won due to the Depression instigating a backlash against the Republicans; even so, some two-thirds of the new Congress was classified as dry.[519] Because Prohibition stretched across party lines, it was clear that a vote for a Democrat did not necessarily equal a vote against Prohibition. Supporting this notion, the Methodist Church Board of Temperance noted that the elections results were "Democratic, rather than wet."[520]

The 1932 Presidential Election

Our country has deliberately undertaken a great social and economic experiment, noble in motive and far reaching in purpose. It must be worked out constructively.
—*President Herbert C. Hoover (R)*[521]

These are President Herbert Hoover's exact words—often incorrectly cited and reduced simply to "Noble Experiment"—that indicate that Hoover hoped to enforce Prohibition during his presidency in a deliberate, nonreactionary and purposeful manner. President Hoover was the first U.S. president truly committed to enforcing Prohibition.[522] In May 1929, Hoover assembled a commission—consisting of current and former judges, cabinet members and university presidents—whose sole purpose was to examine law enforcement and crime related to Prohibition whose findings might help Hoover in making future decisions regarding the policy. With former attorney general George W. Wickersham as chairman of the committee, the Wickersham Commission investigated Prohibition in great detail from May 1929 until its final report was given in January 1931. The final results of this substantial study indicated that the commission was opposed to repeal, was opposed to the restoration of the legalized saloon and was opposed to the proposal to modify the Volstead Act so as to permit manufacture and sale of light wines or beer. Thus, the commission, though successful in the collection of data, had not really presented policy alternatives that could radically improve the enforcement of Prohibition.

By 1932, the economy of the nation had plummeted, and the Great Depression left a multitude of Americans unemployed (an estimated 12.8 million people were unemployed in 1932, about a quarter of the total workforce).[523] Many Americans held Hoover directly responsible for their personal and national condition. Hoover's opponent in 1932 was Franklin

Delano Roosevelt, a popular Democrat and governor of New York who had promised the nation a "New Deal." The Great Depression allowed him to become the odds-on favorite to defeat Hoover in 1932.

In the bleak Depression-era atmosphere, one could legitimately downplay the issue of Prohibition in the election when so many other more pressing social and economic problems persisted. Both Hoover and FDR saw Prohibition as an obstacle to electoral victory that, if possible, would best be ignored.[524] Despite the candidates' desires, however, it was booze and the question of repeal that elicited the greatest and most electric response from the delegates of both parties at each party's national convention. At the Democratic National Convention, renowned philosopher John Dewey exclaimed, "Here we are in the midst of the greatest crisis since the Civil War and the only thing the two national parties seem to want to debate is booze."[525]

Roosevelt and the Democrats endorsed repeal, while Hoover and the Republicans refused to endorse an outright repeal plank.[526] The Republican Party platform called for modification of the Prohibition law, returning the question of Prohibition to the states, while also supporting the continued ban on the saloon. The Democrats' platform on Prohibition was more opportunistic and linked modification of Prohibition to economic recovery. In many respects, this pandering to the public was just good politics. FDR initially favored modifying, but not necessarily repealing, the existing law. One of his primary opponents for the nomination in his party was Maryland's Governor Albert Ritchie, who believed that repeal was the best option. Roosevelt soon realized that repeal would not divide the party, for the convention vote was 934¾ to 213¾ for including a repeal plank in the platform.[527] Ritchie never received more than 23½ delegates (and 16 of those were from Maryland), as the Democrats instead nominated

A famous photo of Franklin D. Roosevelt (D) and Herbert Hoover on Roosevelt's inauguration day, March 4, 1933. *Library of Congress, Prints and Photographs Division, Photograph from Architect of the Capitol, LC-DIG-ppmsca-19179.*

Roosevelt over Ritchie, Al Smith and other contenders.[528] Perhaps ironically, the Democrats' eventual adoption of a wet plank in the official Democratic platform actually cost Ritchie a large number of votes—Ritchie's best promotional tool for himself had now become the official stance of the entire party.

FDR often criticized Hoover's theories on American individualism as being a detriment to how Hoover dealt with the problems associated with the Eighteenth Amendment.[529] One fine example of such criticism occurred in Baltimore in 1932. On the campaign trail, Roosevelt delivered a campaign speech at the Fifth Regiment Armory in Baltimore on October

The Fifth Regiment Armory at 219 Twenty-Ninth Division Street was where Al Smith (1928) and Franklin D. Roosevelt (1932) made campaign speeches highlighting the detriments of Prohibition. *Michael T. Walsh.*

25, just two weeks prior to Election Day. The speech was even broadcast by Columbia Broadcasting Systems (CBS) over the radio, although it was cut short for contractual reasons that allocated only thirty minutes to the speech.[530] A crowd estimated between twelve and fifteen thousand attended in person, not dissimilar to the number who heard Al Smith's speech in Baltimore four years previously.[531] In what the *New York Times* called "the most belligerent speech of his campaign," Roosevelt "attacked" the Republican Party and primarily emphasized Hoover's mishandling of the economic crisis.[532] Roosevelt underscored Hoover's mismanagement of farm relief, foreign trade and America's credit structure. Nevertheless, in the middle of this speech, Roosevelt diverted his attention directly to the issue of Prohibition and how the Hoover administration had failed to successfully deal with the issue and had failed, in his opinion, to effectively articulate its plans for the policy in its official platform.

FDR stated that the "Horseman of Deceit rode when the Republican Convention wrote its plank on prohibition."[533] FDR criticized the quite ambiguous Republican platform for sounding "wet to the wets and dry to the drys." Roosevelt likened this course of action to trying to move "both ways on a one way street," which resulted in a tangle of traffic that made the voter confused in a "dizzy exhibition of uncertainty."[534] Roosevelt then appealed to both wets and drys by proclaiming that "no honest wet and no honest dry can approve of such political tactics."[535] With this appeal to the honest voter, whether wet or dry, Roosevelt may have intended to position himself as the only principled and trustworthy candidate for the voter to choose between. FDR also proclaimed his plan to modify the Volstead Act to "permit States to authorize the manufacture and sale of beer just as fast as the law will let us," with the express purpose of using those potential tax dollars (in this speech FDR uses the figure of $300 million from a beer tax) from sales of liquor in order to prime the declining economy.[536] The crowd in Baltimore "roared" with approval and "cheered point after point in the speech."[537] The *New York Times* even remarked that the "enthusiasm shown for Governor Roosevelt probably was greater than at any other meeting on any of his trips."[538]

The election of 1932 was a landslide victory for Roosevelt. Roosevelt won by 7,060,023, approximately 57 percent of the popular vote.[539] FDR received a resounding 472 Electoral College votes to Hoover's 59. It also served as a major electoral victory for Congressional Democrats, as the Seventy-Third Congress (serving from 1933 to 1935) would control the Senate by 59-36 and the House of Representatives by 313-117.[540] This realigning election of 1932 signaled a new era of dominance by the Democratic Party.

The *Evening Sun* reported that "smashing records on every hand, the voters of Maryland gave the State's electoral votes to Roosevelt by a margin never before approached."[541] Roosevelt's victory over Hoover in Maryland was by a margin of 130,130 votes and 61.5 percent of the popular vote.[542] Roosevelt carried every county in Maryland except Allegany, Garrett and Calvert Counties.[543] Even the Eastern Shore counties, once dry hotbeds that may have been more prone to not vote for the wetter candidate, overwhelmingly voted for Roosevelt. Baltimore City was heavily in favor of Roosevelt (65 percent of the popular vote).[544] Marylanders elected six Democrats to the House of Representatives, as well as wet Democrat Millard Tydings to the Senate, by overwhelming majorities.

The *Evening Sun*'s headline on the day after the November 8 General Election read, "Democrats and Wets Sweep Congress."[545] That headline, in at least some way, might show how the newspaper, and the region that the newspaper served, viewed the importance of Prohibition in the election. Essentially, the headline implies that the wet platform established by the Democrats had helped carry the party to electoral success. It suggests that the election outcome was shaped in some important manner by the issue of Prohibition.

Despite such headlines and general notions, this implication seems to be in error. Certainly, the election results created what some in Maryland saw as an all-but-certain opportunity to at least modify Prohibition. Republican John Philip Hill, who was his party's campaign manager in Maryland in 1932, remarked to the *Evening Sun* that Roosevelt's victory over Hoover "means the great majority of the American people are against the Eighteenth Amendment in any form" and "means the absolute elimination of Federal interference with local State government."[546] Senator Tydings expressed to the *Evening Sun* that it stood to reason that such a victory at the polls meant that legalizing beer would not be surprising in the forthcoming session of Congress.[547] An editorial in the *Evening Sun* urged President-elect Roosevelt to stand by his promise of modifying the Volstead Act "immediately, if not sooner."[548]

Although Prohibition was a campaign issue in 1932, there is a lack of qualitative and very little quantitative evidence that provides support that Prohibition had a significant effect on voter preference in Baltimore or Maryland in 1932. Shannon Lee Parsley stated that "although it cannot be disputed that prohibition was an important issue for many Baltimoreans, its role for determining the contours of the vote in 1932 should not be overstated."[549] Roosevelt's success cannot be attributed to his advocacy of a wet platform, even in a wet city like Baltimore. FDR even won the city wards (Twelfth, Thirteenth, Fifteenth and Sixteenth) with the highest concentration of prohibitionists.[550]

It has been suggested that "in 1932 the force of the Depression moved the entire state toward the Democrats."[551] Marylanders were no different than their counterparts in the other states. The presidential election of 1932 marked a departure from the previous political system dominated by Republicans. Political realignment was occurring, a dynamic change and shift in the electorate toward the Democrats. Although Prohibition was positively an issue of concern among the voters in Maryland, one major overriding issue—the Depression and Hoover's management/mismanagement of that economic crisis—tended to affect voter behavior and, consequently, the election outcomes.[552] Prohibition was an important issue that affected many everyday American lives, but it paled in comparison to how much the Great Depression dramatically affected and substantially altered Americans' lives in the early 1930s.

Chapter 7

TERMINATING THE
"NOBLE EXPERIMENT"

T he election of FDR and the Democratic Party platform, coupled with the effects of the Great Depression, encouraged even the outgoing Congressional members to disassociate themselves from Prohibition. Even before FDR's inauguration in March 1933, Congress had passed the proposed Twenty-First Amendment (votes of 63-23 in the Senate and 289-121 in the House) on February 20, 1933.[553] Section 1 of the Twenty-First Amendment repealed the Eighteenth Amendment of the Constitution. Section 2 stated that "the transportation or importation into any State, Territory, or possession of the United States for delivery or use therein of intoxicating liquors, in violation of the laws thereof, is hereby prohibited."[554] This section basically reimplemented the Webb-Kenyon Act and Reed Amendment, returning the liquor question to the states and treating liquor as a commerce concern.[555] Section 3 provided instructions for ratification of the amendment that would make it the law of the land.

Five representatives in Maryland's House delegation—William P. Cole Jr. (D), Vincent L. Palmisano (D), Ambrose J. Kennedy (D), Stephen W. Gambrill (D) and David J. Lewis (D)—voted for repeal, and one, T. Alan Goldsborough (D), a career dry, voted against it. Senator Tydings (D) voted for repeal, but Senator Goldsborough (R), a suspected dry during his 1928 senatorial campaign against William Cabell Bruce, voted against repeal.[556]

On March 22, 1933, in one of his first major acts in office, Roosevelt signed the Cullen-Harrison bill (also known as the Beer-Wine Revenue Act, or simply the "Beer Bill"), which liberalized the Volstead Act by legalizing the selling and consumption of 3.2 percent alcohol beer.[557] After thirteen years in purgatory, John Barleycorn was about to be (legally) resurrected. The bill was to take effect in most states on April 7, 1933. Maryland was one such state that was set to see the return of legal beer on that April day.

NEW BEER'S EVE IN BALTIMORE

With the date set for beer's return to Baltimore, there was a great need to deal with the many administrative and bureaucratic matters that were essential to support the legal reappearance of beer throughout Maryland. One rather mundane but vitally important issue in need of resolution was the cost of liquor licenses. With a Board of Liquor License Commissioners not yet created in early 1933, the function of selling and distributing licenses would have to be handled by the clerk of the Circuit Court of the county for each county and the clerk of the Court of Common Pleas in Baltimore City.[558] After two weeks of negotiations and arguments, a last-minute agreement resolved the issues, and the local county bills, the city bill and the statewide bill were presented and passed by the Maryland General Assembly on April 5, 1933, as emergency measures.[559] The completed state bill included provisions such as the prices of licenses for hotels, clubs and retail stores; the hours that one could sell beer (no later than 1:00 a.m. in Baltimore City and no Sunday sales, thus implementing a blue law on that day); no sales to minors; and the penalties for failing to purchase a federal wholesaler license if one planned to sell more than five gallons of beer at one time.[560]

Baltimore City and Annapolis were the only two jurisdictions that asked for and received permission to enact "special regulatory measures" with respect to the sale of beer, such as allowing the sale of beer on Sundays in restaurants, clubs and hotels.[561] Other Maryland counties—such as Baltimore, Harford, Prince George's and Caroline—were also exempted from the statewide bill so they could establish their own regulations.[562] Licenses for bars would cost $50 in the city (they were $250 in Baltimore County), and for retail outlets, licenses would be $25.[563] The sale of the licenses enabled Baltimore City to gain immediate revenues of more than $35,000, funds that could have certainly helped the city government's budget.[564]

There were some exemptions in the Beer Bill that allowed several counties to delay the immediate return of the beverage. The General Assembly accepted and approved an exemption offered to it by Carroll County senator J. David Baile that kept 3.2 percent beer illegal in Carroll County for the time being.[565] Carroll County, along with Caroline, Washington and Garrett Counties, would hold a local referendum on the beer issue during the planned special elections of September 12 in which the voters in those counties (except for Garrett County) voted for the return of beer.

Another major issue that needed to be resolved was the beer tax, especially important since the return of legal beer sales was nationally promoted as a means of economic recovery. According to the *Evening Sun*, Baltimore mayor Howard Jackson wanted a Baltimore City beer tax that would be regulatory in nature and not revenue producing. Although excise taxes on beer were seen to be a possible source of revenue, Mayor Jackson opted for taxes that would merely support the inspection and supervision fees of the liquor trade in Baltimore.[566] The key was to get production and sales going as soon as possible to generate enough output that the overall economy might benefit— mainly through an increase in employment opportunities in the beer industry and perhaps also in the government regulation of beer—from beer sales, not just benefit from the taxes applied to the beer. Governor Ritchie signed the bills on April 6, just one day before beer's return. By July 1933, Baltimore City had collected about $175,000 in revenue from beer licenses and taxes combined—although it's not clear whether this sum was used per Mayor Jackson's request at inspection and supervision or if this was pure revenue. Nevertheless, in July 1933, Baltimore was one of the leading cities, listed as second only to Philadelphia (which had an astounding $725,000) by the *Evening Sun*, in the collection of revenue from beer sales.[567]

The return of beer to the Maryland region in April 1933 sparked renewed interest in advertising for beer. Gunther's Brewery and the Globe Brewery advertised their product's return heavily in the days before and after April 7. Gunther's Brewery ran a rather large ad in the *Afro-American* that asked Baltimore and Maryland "Is Everybody Happy?" now that "the fight is over! You won! You got your BEER! And your beer is Gunther's Beer!"[568] The ad pictured a man pleasantly sleeping, dreaming of a frothing, foaming beer. An Arrow beer ad in the *Afro-American* in April 1933 also advertises the April 7 delivery in order to reacquaint oneself with "the best beer in town!"[569] A&P grocery stores advertised in the *Evening Sun* on April 6 that they would have local beer, both Gunther's and the Globe's Arrow, available once the clock struck midnight.[570] They regretted the fact that Baltimore's Beer Bill did not allow all of their stores to stock beer but informed potential customers that their local A&P store would deliver the beer "anywhere in Baltimore City" for two dollars per case and deposit.[571]

A 2017 photograph of the renovated Gunther's Brewery complex. The brewery is now home to Gunther & Company restaurant, which proudly embraces the buildings' brewing history. *Michael T. Walsh.*

Perhaps one of the most famous advertisements against Prohibition in Baltimore is the prominent sign painted on a Fell's Point building that clearly reads, "Vote Against Prohibition." The sign, painted sometime in 1932 or 1933, is still visible today, and while its purpose is easily discernible, the advertiser or advocacy group that painted it remains lost to history. Despite this fact, the public sign tends to represent the anti-prohibition sentiments of Baltimoreans as repeal became an impending reality in 1933. Certainly, Baltimoreans later obeyed that sign's demand in the September 12, 1933 special elections.

Editorial cartoons in this era were particularly successful at presenting particular viewpoints of not only the cartoonist but also the general sentiment of the readership. On April 3, 1933, a cartoon by *Sun* cartoonist Edmund Duffy entitled "It's Been a Long Time Getting Here—So" depicted a giant frothy glass of beer with a sign underneath that reads, "Handle with Care." In the coming days, Duffy, who had come to the *Sun* in 1924, would use his cartoons to generally show his emotions toward the impending return of

The iconic "Vote Against Prohibition" sign in Fell's Point at the corner of Shakespeare and Broadway Streets. *Michael T. Walsh.*

beer and the gradual move toward repeal of the Eighteenth Amendment—emotions that might have been shared by a sizable number of Baltimore's population. On April 5, Duffy drew a cartoon entitled "Repeal—Try Your Aim" that depicted a furious "Mr. Dry" (by then a well-known illustration) being pelted with a cannonball that was named "Michigan Vote," in obvious reference to Michigan's state convention being on the verge of ratifying the Twenty-First Amendment. In another example of a political cartoon espousing the ideas and views of its author, Duffy's cartoon from April 9, 1933, was entitled "The Exile." In this illustration, "Mr. Dry" is seen standing on a small rock island clutching his always visible umbrella in one hand and a book, *The Life of Napoleon*, in the other, staring at a brewery that is open for business on the distant shore. Duffy suggests here that the drys had fought their Waterloo, ultimately lost and now would be cast away to Saint Helena.[572]

Baltimore newspapers portrayed most Baltimoreans as being happy about the anticipated return of beer on April 7. Patrolman Nicholas W. Dieter, expressing his joy that Prohibition was nearing its end, re-erected a flagpole at his house on North Potomac Street and flew the U.S. flag, which had not been flown since Prohibition went into effect.[573] Mr. Adam Fleckenstein braved long lines at city hall to become the first person in Baltimore City to obtain a beer license for his saloon on Chase Street.[574] Bartenders even put in a bid to reorganize the bartenders' union, the Beverage Dispenser's Union 532, which had disbanded in 1922.[575] Baltimoreans were rapidly trying to prepare themselves for a celebration that would make New Year's Eve look tame by comparison.[576] In fact, the *Sun* even referred to April 6 as "New Beer's Eve."[577] Baltimore planned on having a seriously raucous party of enormous proportions, not to be rivaled by any celebrations in Baltimore's past.

The day before the return of beer, Baltimore's parks board must have realized that the return of beer and the imminent demise of Prohibition was a historical event that deserved to be memorialized. The board created what has come to be dubbed the "Repeal Statue," a sculpted stone panel that some purport to depict cherubs operating a still with corn and grapes, located on the grounds of the board's old headquarters north of the Druid Hill Park gateway on Baltimore's Madison Avenue. The "statue" was donated by Baltimore businessman William Parker (who helped build Baltimore's famed Emerson Hotel in downtown Baltimore and later became the hotel's managing director) to the Board of Park Commissioners in 1932. According to Parker's son, the panel may not have been originally meant to serve as a memorial to repeal. The son, William H. Parker Jr., has indicated that his father was more likely to have been a prohibitionist and was even friends with Billy Sunday.[578] However, despite this claim, the elder Parker also had an invested stake in the Emerson Hotel and may have realized the possible profitability of the return of beer and potential repeal of Prohibition. Whatever Parker's true intentions may have been, upon the statue's dedication on April 6, 1933, Parks Superintendent Leroy Nichols remarked that the memorial will be "set among the earthworks thrown up in the park during the Civil War" to celebrate the "battle waged for the return of legal beer."[579] The "Repeal Statue" remains in its place to this day near Druid Hill Park.

On Friday, April 7, 1933, despite the rainy weather, Baltimore officially welcomed beer back to town and gave it a "gay and noisy welcome."[580] The *Sun* and the *Evening Sun* extensively covered the events that unfolded in Baltimore at midnight. The newspapers heralded the turning on of beer spigots all over the city in hotels and bars such as the New Howard and Rennert Hotels as a sign that a new era—"the new deal"—had commenced in Baltimore.[581] And the reactions of Baltimore City to the return of beer were quite incredible. Crowds gathered outside the Gunther and Globe breweries as beer trucks took their shipments to their destinations.[582] Huge celebrations were held at area hotels and newly reopened saloons, where more than seventy-five thousand glasses of real beer were poured for crowds of every element of Baltimore society.[583] The celebration continued over the weekend as thousands of glasses were poured in private homes and the Lyric Theater became Baltimore's first theater to open a bar for its patrons, who were attending a Bach sonata.[584] A delegation of brewers from Baltimore, Milwaukee and Washington presented President Roosevelt with cases of the newly legalized beer as a token of appreciation for ending the drought.[585]

The renowned "Repeal Statue," located near the Druid Hill Park gate entrance on the corner of Madison Avenue and Cloverdale Road. *Michael T. Walsh.*

An April 8 editorial in the *Sun* enthusiastically proclaimed the following:

> *Beer is back with a bang, but without a headache. The prodigal beverage, Which has been wandering for thirteen years in the outer darkness of illegality, returned to the taprooms yesterday with the law's blessing, and thousands of customers turned out to see the slaying of the fatted calf and to join in slaking their thirst with drafts of the new brew. It was a happy occasion. And it was solemnized in a decent and proper fashion.*[586]

Despite the ebullient celebration by Baltimoreans, no arrests were made in the morning hours of April 7.[587] An unattributed editorial in the *Baltimore Sun* stated that there were not any "unseemly developments yesterday to mar the first full day of the more liberal dispensation upon which we are fortunately entering."[588] Police Commissioner Gaither ordered speakeasies to open their doors and apply for beer licenses. The speakeasies seemed to oblige with little resistance, perhaps realizing that their financial fortune might possibly improve through the sales of legal beer.[589] Arrests for drunkenness in Baltimore for the first month of legal beer were actually fewer (305) than during the same period in 1932 (315).[590]

Local Baltimore County newspaper the *Catonsville Herald and Baltimore Countian* reported that legalizing beer would prove to be good for the local and national economy. The return of the 3.2 percent beer industry would create a simultaneous rise in profit for other industries as well. Hotels could potentially regain their customers from the speakeasies, and women could find work making pretzels, a popular snack enjoyed by beer drinkers and a product that would surely need to have a higher output now that beer was back.[591] Showing that Baltimore's tradition of crabs and beer is not merely the work of present-day tourist guides, the *Herald* stated that "crab fishermen of Chesapeake Bay are getting double prices for all they can catch. Beer and crabmeat seem to go together."[592] That winning combination remains today a steady staple in a Baltimorean's diet! The newspaper also claimed that in the first few weeks since beer returned, drunkenness and arrests had decreased in the local area.[593] This claim initially debunked the drys' belief that re-legalizing alcohol would only accelerate America's decline into mass drunkenness.

Beer returned to most of the United States in April 1933. But the repeal of the Eighteenth Amendment was not yet complete. There was still unfinished business to attend to. The final act that would forever terminate the constitutional prohibition of alcohol was about to commence.

RATIFICATION OF THE TWENTY-FIRST AMENDMENT

Whereas the Eighteenth Amendment was ratified by the state legislatures, the Twenty-First Amendment would be ratified by state conventions. Congress mandated that these conventions, rather than the state legislatures, would vote since "state legislatures were notoriously dry being dominated by rural, fundamentalist interests, passionate in their defense of Prohibition" and were presumably more prone to the influence and pressures applied by groups such as the ASL.[594] The state convention delegates were to be popularly elected by qualified voters.

In Maryland, Governor Ritchie praised Congress's action by stating that it was "a great victory for the ideals of the people of Maryland."[595] Most wets believed that the state convention method of ratification would be a better and more accurate representation of how Maryland's citizenry, and not just its legislators, viewed the Eighteenth Amendment. For Maryland, the election of delegates to the state convention that would vote on the Twenty-First Amendment was to be held on September 12, 1933. In April 1933, Maryland's General Assembly named a twenty-nine-member nominating committee (one from each of Maryland's twenty-three counties and one from each of Baltimore's six legislative districts) chosen to nominate the convention candidates who would appear on the ballot for the special election.[596] This committee convened in Annapolis on June 21, 1933, to begin the nominations, which had to be complete by August 1. Three delegates were to be chosen from each of Maryland's six Congressional districts (eighteen delegates), plus there would be an additional six delegates chosen from the state at large, providing a total of twenty-four delegates. Baltimore City was split between four Congressional districts. This gerrymandered split was advantageous to the city, especially on the particular issue of Prohibition.

The committee was to nominate these candidates to three separate sets for the convention: one set pledged to vote for repeal, the second set pledged to vote against repeal and the third set was unpledged.[597] Therefore, the physical ballot for the popular election on September 12 would feature nine delegates pledged to repeal, nine who were dry and nine who were neither.[598] The voters of each district would then cast their ballots for the entire slate of delegates in their own Congressional district and in the state at large that best represented their own views toward repeal. The candidates who received the highest number of votes within the winning set (twenty-four total delegates) would then represent Maryland during the ratification process in the state convention, due to be held on October 18, 1933.

The *Sun*'s September 12 edition reminded Marylanders to "be sure to vote" to ensure that "Maryland's long championship of repeal…be followed by a victory at the polls."[599] TABLE 9 represents the *Evening Sun*'s early (not final) results of the election in Maryland as of September 13, 1933. The final state vote tally (250,906 votes), using the only extant or available final voting numbers from the November 8, 1933 edition of the *New York Times*, shows that Maryland's votes for repeal (205,130, or 81.8 percent) greatly outweighed its votes against repeal (45,776, or 18 percent).[600] Thus, Maryland favored repeal by a nearly five-to-one margin.[601] In Baltimore, the vote was nearly ten to one in favor of repeal,[602] and not one of the city's 672 precincts returned a vote against repeal.[603] At eight polling places, no dry votes were cast, and in eighteen other polling places, only one dry vote was cast at each. The Forty-Fourth Precinct, in the central business district, had the best showing for the drys, with repeal still favored at sixty to one, and the Twenty-Eighth Ward proved to be the driest as well, with repeal prevailing at only a four-to-one ratio (a still robust 81.9 percent in favor of repeal).[604] The *Sun* reported that the city's ratio equaled the ratios of Chicago, Milwaukee, Boston and Providence, all of which were second only to St. Louis's twenty-to-one ratio of wet majorities in the United States' largest cities.[605] In comparing Baltimore's 1916 Prohibition referendum to the September 12 special election, one sees that the public sentiment against Prohibition, already substantial at about 74 percent in 1916, had increased in 1933 to just shy of 90 percent. The Eastern Shore, "long regarded by the Anti-Saloon League as its private dominion," had two counties, Somerset (50.1 percent against) and Dorchester (55 percent against) vote against repeal. All of the other Eastern Shore counties voted for repeal.[606]All of the delegates elected for the convention were wet and were pledged to vote for repeal. Not one delegate was voted into the delegation to support Prohibition.

In four Maryland counties—Caroline, Carroll, Washington and Garrett—local referendums were also voted on during this special election that pertained to the sale of beer, which had been legalized in other areas of the state in April.[607] Caroline (60.5 percent) and Carroll (57 percent) Counties voted for the sale of beer, and Garrett County narrowly voted against it (51.3 percent dry), whereas Washington County voted to repeal Prohibition and the local option laws that were in effect (70.8 percent).[608] Interestingly, although Garrett County rejected the return of beer, the county did narrowly vote for repeal (49.7 percent versus 47.2 percent against), suggesting that the county's residents were somewhat unresolved in their convictions on alcohol regulation. A *Sun* editorial from September 1933 stated that "the verdict the Free State has now returned is the same verdict which the people of Maryland have proclaimed informally almost from the inception of the national Prohibition movement."[609]

Anti-Saloon League superintendent George W. Crabbe expressed his views to the *Sun* on the overwhelming vote for repeal of the Eighteenth Amendment in Maryland. Crabbe said that the Anti-Saloon League would continue "to fight the re-establishment of saloons in local communities," essentially admitting that the Prohibition cause must return to its roots of local options in smaller communities.[610] Crabbe then also added that "so many friends failed to vote on the grounds that experience with the saloon will give the people the lesson and fact necessary to end it forever."[611]

Yale Law School scholar Ethan Davis stated that "the ratification of the Twenty-first Amendment might be called one of the most democratic moments in American history....Almost all voters in America had the unprecedented opportunity to bless or condemn a federal Constitutional

Amendment directly."[612] This once-in-a-lifetime opportunity for American voters, however, had mixed results in terms of the polling itself. Despite the election outcomes, voter turnout in Maryland, as it was in other states across the nation for these special elections, was rather low.[613] Baltimore's voter turnout was less than one would expect, considering how wet the city was—only a little over one-third (126,197 out of 336,132) of the registered voters cast their ballots at the polls. The *Sun* reported that only about half of Anne Arundel County's registered voters cast their ballots in comparison to those county voters who voted in the presidential election of 1932.[614] Anonymous dry leaders in Maryland stated in the *New York Times* that the anti-repeal vote "suffered from the wet and cloudy weather" across the state during Election Day.[615] The low voter turnout is perplexing considering how much Prohibition and repeal populated politics, policy, news and everyday life in America and especially in Maryland. Bad weather on Election Day could not have been the only reason such low voter turnout occurred; however, it is the only evidence available that distinctly explains such a low number without succumbing to mere historical speculation. It remains a mystery why voter turnout on such a hot-button issue that clearly captured the public's attention over the preceding thirteen years was so abysmal.

On October 18, 1933, Maryland's twenty-four elected delegates, all pledged to vote for repeal, met at the statehouse in Annapolis, Maryland, to deliver the "rubber stamp" on repeal.[616] Governor Ritchie was in attendance to witness history—a day he might have thought would never arrive. R. Bennett Darnall of Ruxton (Baltimore County) served as president over these proceedings and addressed the delegates:

> *The Eighteenth Amendment…affects directly the life and habits of the people. It has no place in the Constitution. It brought about much suffering and corruption, and has made a nation of whiskey drinkers.…I am sure you feel, as I do, that it is a distinct privilege and a very great pleasure to represent the people of our State in ratifying their mandate in voting of the repeal of the Eighteenth Amendment. We are happy in voting today to undo this wrong.…We should do all in our power to bring about true temperance and advise for legislation that will bring sane and well-regulated handling of the liquor so that the conditions that prevailed prior to Prohibition and which may have been largely responsible for it, will not return.*[617]

Darnall's speech was a typical wet political speech, openly welcoming forms of temperance without the need of total Prohibition. It represented the attitudes of many of his fellow delegates and most of the people of Maryland in 1933: alcohol was fine in moderation, but a return to the era where "tied house" saloons were believed to disrupt the physical and mental health of Americans was not welcome and should not be encouraged in any shape or form. Other delegates who had the opportunity to speak reiterated the points that the state convention mechanism was a show of true democracy, a victory for local self-rule and one devoid of party politics, as the delegates did not represent parties but rather represented a philosophy and an ideal instead.[618] The resolution to repeal the Eighteenth Amendment through adopting the Twenty-First Amendment was soon voted on through a roll call vote at 3:20 p.m.[619] The vote for repeal was unanimous. Maryland became the twenty-seventh state to reject national Prohibition.[620]

REPEAL ARRIVES: DECEMBER 5, 1933

As state conventions met throughout the late summer and early fall of 1933, the all but inevitable repeal of Prohibition meant that Prohibition Bureau headquarters in the states could begin to downsize and close their facilities. In Baltimore, that meant closing down an annex at Fort McHenry, where a two-story building just off Fort McHenry's main grounds served as Prohibition headquarters in Baltimore. This was where Prohibition agents kept their offices and congregated before and after raids. In July 1933, sixty Prohibition agents were on duty at the headquarters. By August, only twenty-five remained.[621] By December, the office had been entirely vacated by Prohibition forces and replaced by the Weather Bureau.[622] The closing of Prohibition headquarters pleased one anonymous writer at the *Evening Sun* who had hoped in September that "getting the place cleaned and fumigated by Christmas would be a pleasant Christmas gift for the people of Maryland."[623]

On December 5, 1933, after Utah became the thirty-sixth state to ratify the Twenty-First Amendment, President Roosevelt gave Presidential Proclamation 2065, which made the repeal of the Eighteenth Amendment official.[624] Legal distilled spirits and wine quickly reappeared in Maryland on December 6. The text stated that the Eighteenth Amendment was repealed due to the "conventions in thirty-six States of the United States, constituting three-fourths of the whole number of the States had ratified the said repeal amendment."[625] Roosevelt also noted that he hoped for cooperation by Americans in ensuring that this regained individual freedom would not be "accompanied by the repugnant conditions obtained prior to the adoption of the Eighteenth Amendment and those that have existed since its adoption."[626] He said that the return of the saloon, in its old form or in some "modern guise," and its attendant potential for "social and political evils" would not be tolerated by his administration—nor, he hoped, by the American public. FDR hoped that the ratification of the Twenty-First Amendment and the return of taxable liquor for government purposes would aid in "good government, law, and order" and "not be a detriment to health, morals, and social integrity."[627] It was the right message at the exact right time for the Depression-ravaged America.

One of the *Evening Sun*'s headlines read, "Headaches Few as City Greets Return of Liquor."[628] The *Evening Sun* also asserted that, as they had in April, "Baltimoreans, generally speaking…kept their heads last night."[629] With the return of liquor, it was also announced that the Gwynnbrook Distillery in Owings Mills would reopen for the first time since it stopped producing medicinal liquors in 1921.[630] For many folks, happy days were indeed here again.

At least one company used the occasion of repeal to commemorate the fall of Prohibition. Stewart & Company, a well-known department store in Baltimore with a large customer base among middle- and upper-income residents, published an ad in December 1933 that used the end of Prohibition as a marketing ploy to attract customers to its store. Stewart's opened a new shop—entitled the "Repeal Corner"—on the third floor of its department store "dedicated to those who intend to celebrate the repeal."[631] The goods that were to be sold included cocktail shakers, drinking glasses and "everything that goes to make the party a howling success."[632]

Although Prohibition had ended, the new regulations on liquor were much tougher and more stringent than they had been before 1920.[633] There were stricter requirements for obtaining liquor licenses, such as the required signature of the property owner in order to have a license.[634] In all, there were twenty-nine forms of liquor licenses.[635] Under the statewide liquor control bill, "regulations for the sale of whisky, wines, and beer" varied greatly throughout the state. Garrett County was still dry, yet St. Mary's County was liberal in granting liquor licenses at minimal fees.[636] Baltimore City could sell unrestricted amounts of whiskey in hotels, but Cecil County allowed the sale of only one quart to a guest.[637] Even on the day before

Stewart & Company Department Store, at 226–32 West Lexington Street, housed the "Repeal Corner" in December 1933. *Baltimore Museum of Industry, Baltimore Gas & Electric Company Photographic Collection, BGE.5260N.*

the official repeal, the *Evening Sun* reported that the only available "whisky" might turn out to be bootleg.[638]

The return of liquor in December 1933 certainly invigorated the legal and local liquor market in Baltimore County and infused those liquor businesses with revenue. Baltimore County liquor sales during the Christmas season totaled almost $250,000.[639] Also noteworthy, the county police reported that "little disorder and drunkenness" occurred, despite the "tremendous sale of liquors."[640] An infusion of revenue and no discernible poor public behavior provided hope in those early days that repeal would be a success.

From the late nineteenth century through 1920, some Americans thought that Prohibition was the answer to uplifting and reforming an increasingly dysfunctional society. Paradoxically, by 1933, with the nation in the midst of the Great Depression, most American citizens had hoped that a *repeal* of Prohibition would boost/reform a depressed society. Despite some successful reforms in the drinking habits of some Americans, the enforcement—though not necessarily the policy itself—of Prohibition ultimately failed to attain its stated long-term objective of a dry America for future generations. The "Noble Experiment" had been terminated.

"MARYLAND, MY MARYLAND:" CONCLUSIONS AND HANGOVERS

Our story of Prohibition in Baltimore and Maryland hereby ends with the ratification and subsequent repeal of the Twenty-First Amendment. Never again would there be a constitutional amendment that outlawed the transportation, distribution and manufacture of alcoholic beverages in the United States. But although the story arc for this book ends with this event, one could say that Prohibition gave America a bit of a hangover that still persists to this day in many respects. In early 2005, Juanita Duggan, executive vice-president and chief executive of the Wine and Spirits Wholesalers of America, stated that "instead of thinking that our history is in the past and ended with the repeal of Prohibition, you need to think of it as being present,"[641] suggesting that dismissing the past and the lessons that one can glean from it is an all-too-common practice.

There could be a whole other book dedicated to revealing how Prohibition has left a lasting impression on American society, including the culture, society and political institutions in Maryland. The history of the Prohibition era in Maryland continues to be kept alive and in the mainstream public conscious through celebrations of "Repeal Day" every December 5 in area bars. The reemergence of pre-Prohibition liqueurs and cocktails along with faux-speakeasies throughout the United States (including a few in Baltimore and Maryland) have provided modern bar patrons and "hipsters" alike with a certain chic nostalgia for the old saloon. The proliferation of new breweries and wineries throughout Baltimore and Maryland possibly signifies a coming renaissance for the city's and state's brewing and wine industry. Even the current revival of Maryland's once-proud rye whiskey industry, signified most notably by the current popularity of Sagamore Spirit Distillery (owned by Under Armour CEO Kevin Plank and located in Baltimore's waterfront Port Covington neighborhood), is slowly but surely finding a niche audience with hopeful aspirations for more mass expansion and production in the future. References to Maryland's strong pre-Prohibition distilling history are a great marketing ploy for these new distilleries that hope to capitalize on historical reminiscences of Prohibition as well as a great-tasting product.[642]

Remarkably, public enchantment with the Prohibition era in Maryland has even engendered a Prohibition-themed museum shop. The 2016 opening of the McLhinney Speakeasy Museum and International Market in Havre de Grace, Maryland, gives its patrons an opportunity to discover and explore the subject of Prohibition.[643] Maryland's first speakeasy museum aims to preserve and promote the history of Prohibition in that Maryland town through stories, pictures, tours and collections. The museum building itself, complete with original "Prohibition bars" on the backdoor, was an old newsstand, owned then and now by the McLhinney family, that was stationed next door to a 1920s speakeasy.[644] Future restorations, particularly of that speakeasy, are expected in the coming years.

The shadowy ghost of Prohibition has, at times, loomed large over modern American life. One of the many legacies Prohibition has bestowed on later generations is that of the lack of uniformity in America's liquor laws. The local option vote has allowed many local areas in the United States to remain dry. The idea of a local option law through public referendum, as the primary method of implementing alcohol prohibition, is once again the preference of contemporary reformers. In a 2010 *USA Today* article, it was reported that one in nine counties in the United States is still presently dry.[645] Until 2013, the state of Maryland itself still had a dry town due to the adoption of local option laws. The town of Damascus (population 12,396) in Montgomery County, which not surprisingly has Methodist roots, had been dry since 1884 (local option) and had rejected numerous referendums to repeal the local law in 1933, 1976, 1984, 1992 and 1996.[646] During the election of 2012, the residents of the town finally elected (66 percent voted for the referendum) to allow alcohol sales at restaurants.[647]

Duggan's 2005 quote itself was directly related to the 5-4 Supreme Court decision in *Granholm v. Heald* (2005) that ruled that direct shipment of wine to out-of-state consumers—should an individual state choose to do so—was constitutional and did not violate Section 2 of the Twenty-First Amendment.[648] Despite the 2005 ruling, the direct sale of wine was not allowed in Maryland until July 1, 2011, and even then only in limited fashion from wine manufacturer to consumer and not directly from wine retailer to consumer so as not to alter the three-tier alcohol distribution system too much. Constant (and sometimes erroneous) analogies made between Prohibition and America's War on Drugs, the twenty-first-century epidemic of opioid abuse (especially in Maryland) or even the public debates

McLhinney's Speakeasy Museum and International Market opened in Havre de Grace, Maryland, in 2016, celebrating the history of Prohibition in a town once known as "Little Chicago." *Michael T. Walsh.*

over smoking bans in Maryland have all, in some way or another, drawn comparisons and contrasts to the Prohibition policy.

In many ways, Prohibition has come to typify and define an entire decade, the 1920s, as this era has been memorialized in all types of popular media, from radio to television to the silver screen and now to the Internet. It is thus no surprise that Prohibition continues to be relevant to some of today's hot topic discussions and continues to intrigue Americans as well. One hopes that the story of Prohibition in Baltimore and Maryland strengthened that public fascination and may have stimulated even greater interest and appreciation for the rich and unique history of Prohibition in the "Free State."

TABLES

TABLE 1. Voting Results for the 1916 Prohibition Referendum in Baltimore City's Wards

Ward	Total Population	% Against Prohibition
1	33,257	97.7
2	20,823	89.2
3	19,270	89.4
4	14,987	82.8
5	17,604	85.9
6	31,077	78.9
7	33,038	80.5
8	37,292	74.3
9	31,087	66.3
10	20,225	85.0
11	21,376	68.1
12	36,103	56.2
13	33,660	54.5
14	25,201	67.8
15	48,134	54.5
16	35,436	54.6
17	20,636	70.7
18	20,183	76.6
19	23,678	68.2

Ward	Total Population	% Against Prohibition
20	36,851	72.8
21	19,423	82.2
22	15,008	78.9
23	16,599	80.6
24	24,584	78.0
25	17,360	*
26	36,873	*
27	36,153	*
28	7,908	*
TOTALS	**733,826**	**74.7 (average)**

No voting results for Wards 25 through 28 since these wards were not annexed until 1918.

TABLE 2. Baltimore's Religious Populations, 1916

Type	Total Size
Roman Catholic	137,730
Protestant Episcopal	17,209
Presbyterian	9,984
Lutheran	17,655
Baptist	33,511
Jewish	11,775
Congregationalist	0
Methodist	41,784
Other	26,951
TOTAL	**296,599**

TABLE 3. 1922 *Literary Digest* National Poll

Polls	Present Enforcement	%	Modification	%	Repeal	%	TOTALS
Main	306,255	38.5	325,549	41.1	164,453	20.4	796,257
Women's	48,485	44.5	39,914	36.7	20,448	18.8	108,847
Factory	1,453	8.4	10,871	62.1	4,955	29.5	17,279
TOTALS	356,193		376,334		189,856		922,383

TABLE 4. 1922 *Literary Digest* National Poll: Men vs. Women

Gender	Present Enforcement	%	Modification	%	Repeal	%
Men	307,708	37.8	336,420	41.4	169,408	20.8
Women	48,485	44.5	39,914	36.7	20,448	18.8

Gender	Present Enforcement and/or Modification	%	Repeal and/or Modification	%
Men	644,128	79.2	205,828	62.2
Women	88,399	81.2	60,362	55.5

TABLE 5. 1922 *Literary Digest* Poll: Maryland Men vs. Women

Polls	Present Enforcement	%	Modification	%	Repeal	%
Men	2,765	27.9	3,618	36.5	3,722	37.5
Women	486	32.6	537	36.0	466	31.3
TOTALS	3,251		4,155		4,188	

Polls	Present Enforcement and/or Modification	%	Repeal and/or Modification	%	TOTALS
Men	6,383	63.2	7,340	72.6	10,105
Women	1,023	68.7	1,003	67.4	1,489
TOTALS	7,406		8,343		11,594

TABLE 6. "Izzie" Einstein's Observations (1923)

City	Time to Acquire Alcohol
New Orleans	35 seconds
Detroit	3 minutes
New York	3 minutes, 10 seconds
Boston	11 minutes
Pittsburgh	14 minutes
Atlanta	17 minutes
Baltimore	**18 minutes, 20 seconds**
Chicago	21 minutes
St. Louis	21 minutes
Cleveland	29 minutes
Minneapolis	31 minutes
Washington, D.C.	2 hours, 8 minutes

TABLE 7. Percent Increase in Drinking and Driving Arrests in American Cities (1919–25)

City	Percent (%)
Akron, Ohio	248%
Atlanta, Georgia	91%
Baltimore, Maryland	**96%**
Boston, Massachusetts	383%
Chicago, Illinois	476%
Detroit, Michigan	50%
Duluth, Minnesota	457%
Hartford, Connecticut	614%
Milwaukee, Wisconsin	3,209%
Minneapolis, Minnesota	1,054%
New Haven, Connecticut	753%
Newton, Massachusetts	185%

City	Percent (%)
New York, New York	491%
Portland, Oregon	148%
Providence, Rhode Island	283%
Spokane, Washington	413%
Springfield, Massachusetts	368%
Trenton, New Jersey	331%
Washington, D.C.	383%
Worcester, Massachusetts	408%

TABLE 8. Arrests for Prohibition Violations in Baltimore City, 1917–34
(Percentages Rounded to the Nearest Tenth)

Type	1917	1918	1919	1920	1921	1922
Total Arrests	49,147	62,076	50,027	41,988	54,602	60,947
Prohibition Law	0	0	0	0	344	623
Drunkenness	5,129	7,552	5,096	1,785	3,258	4,955
Prohibition Law % of Total Arrests	0	0	0	0	0.60%	1.00%
Drunkenness % of Total Arrests	10.40%	12.20%	10.20%	4.30%	6.00%	8.10%
Combined % of Total Arrests	10.40%	12.20%	10.20%	4.30%	6.60%	9.10%

Type	1923	1924	1925	1926	1927	1928
Total Arrests	74,295	88,307	94,521	96,924	108,745	110,219
Prohibition Law	861	No data	1,124	564	1,172	1,115
Drunkenness	6,235	No data	5,687	5,755	5,475	5,778
Prohibition Law % of Total Arrests	1.20%	No data	1.20%	0.60%	1.10%	1.00%
Drunkenness % of Total Arrests	8.40%	No data	6.00%	5.90%	5.00%	5.20%
Combined % of Total Arrests	9.60%	No data	7.20%	6.50%	6.10%	6.20%

Type	1929	1930	1931	1932	1933	1934
Total Arrests	119,021	116,151	125,621	115,290	102,741	99,743
Prohibition Law	1,145	937	1,329	1,382	536	0
Drunkenness	5,420	5,260	4,980	4,600	4,264	3,711
Prohibition Law % of Total Arrests	0.90%	0.80%	1.10%	1.20%	0.50%	0%
Drunkenness % of Total Arrests	4.60%	4.50%	4.00%	4.00%	4.20%	3.70%
Combined % of Total Arrests	5.50%	5.30%	5.10%	5.20%	4.70%	3.70%

TABLE 9. Counties in Maryland and the September 12 Referendum as of 9/13/1933
(Percentages Rounded to the Nearest Tenth)

County	For Repeal	Against Repeal	Total Votes	% For Repeal	% Against Repeal
Allegany	10,279	2,192	12,646	81.3%	17.3%
Anne Arundel	6,401	1,076	7,626	83.9%	14.1%
Baltimore City	119,019	11,295	132,399	89.9%	8.5%
Baltimore County	17,225	2,768	20,412	84.4%	13.6%
Calvert	772	221	1,109	69.6%	19.9%
Caroline	1,339	967	2,343	57.1%	41.3%
Carroll	3,570	2,900	6,507	54.9%	44.6%
Cecil	1,925	1,492	3,417	56.3%	43.7%
Charles	997	81	1,114	89.5%	7.3%
Dorchester	1,132	1,409	2,562	44.2%	55.0%
Frederick	6,132	3,282	9,436	65.0%	34.8%
Garrett	1,475	1,400	2,967	49.7%	47.2%
Harford	625	158	813	76.9%	19.4%
Howard	2,150	651	2,801	76.8%	23.2%
Kent	1,493	791	2,330	64.1%	33.9%
Montgomery	6,199	2,891	9,111	68.0%	31.7%

County	For Repeal	Against Repeal	Total Votes	% For Repeal	% Against Repeal
Prince George's	5,889	1,352	7,357	80.0%	18.4%
Queen Anne's	1,216	467	1,792	67.9%	26.1%
Somerset	1,030	1,074	2,142	48.1%	50.1%
St. Mary's	1,764	96	1,860	94.8%	5.2%
Talbot	1,761	919	2,680	65.7%	34.3%
Washington	6,399	2,477	8,891	72.0%	27.9%
Wicomico	2,314	2,009	4,323	53.5%	46.5%
Worcester	1,342	866	2,208	60.8%	39.2%
TOTALS	**202,448**	**42,834**	**248,846**	**81.4%**	**17.2%**

NOTES

Introduction

1. Walsh, "Wet and Dry in the Land of Pleasant Living."

Chapter 1

2. Johnson et al., *Sun Papers of Baltimore*, 389.

3. Clark, *Deliver Us from Evil*, 5–6.

4. Lichtman, *Prejudice and the Old Politics*, 77.

5. For example, see Bader, *Prohibition in Kansas*; Lerner, *Dry Manhattan*; Kavieff, *Violent Years*; Allsop, *Bootleggers*; Peck, *Prohibition in Washington, D.C.*; and Murphy, "Bootlegging Mothers and Drinking Daughters," 174–94.

6. For example, see Lerner, *Dry Manhattan*, and Kavieff, *Violent Years*.

7. Olson, *Baltimore*, 331.

8. Pegram, "Temperance Politics and Regional Political Culture," 58.

9. United States Census Bureau, *Census of Population and Housing, 1920*, vol. 1, *Population, 1920*—number and distribution of inhabitants. See https://www.census.gov/prod/www/decennial.html.

10. Ibid., *Census of Population and Housing, 1930*, vol. 1, 1,268—number and distribution of inhabitants. Total population for states, counties and townships or other minor civil divisions; for urban and rural areas; and for cities and other incorporated places. See https://www.census.gov/prod/www/decennial.html.

11. Byse, "Alcoholic Beverage Control before Repeal," 558.
12. Brugger, *Maryland*, 407, 456.

Chapter 2

13. *Baltimore Sun*, January 18, 1920.
14. Andrews, *History of Maryland*, 197.
15. *Foundation, Progress, and Principles*, 1.
16. Blocker, *American Temperance Movements*, 41.
17. Ibid.
18. Gusfield, *Symbolic Crusade*, 49.
19. Andrews, *History of Maryland*, 472.
20. *New York Times*, February 3, 1896.
21. Andrews, *History of Maryland*, 472; Scharf, *Chronicles of Baltimore*, 124.
22. W. Wayne Smith, "Politics and Democracy in Maryland, 1800–1854," in Walsh and Fox, *Maryland*, 304.
23. Ibid.
24. Dale P. Van Wieren, "Chronology of the American Brewing Industry," *American Breweries II* (1998–2000), http://www.beerhistory.com/library/holdings/chronology.shtml.
25. Partisan Historical Society, "Prohibition Presidential/Vice-Presidential Candidates 1872–Present," http://www.prohibitionists.org/History/votes/votes.html.
26. Dave Leip, "1896 Presidential General Election Results," *Atlas of U.S. Presidential Elections*, http://uselectionatlas.org/RESULTS/national.php?year=1896.
27. U.S. Supreme Court, *Mugler v. Kansas*.
28. Anderson, "Direct Shipment of Wine."
29. U.S. Supreme Court, Wilson Original Package Act (1890), https://www.law.cornell.edu/uscode/text/27/121.
30. Link and McCormick, *Progressivism*, 103.
31. Hamm, *Shaping the Eighteenth Amendment*, 21.
32. Burnham, "New Perspectives on the Prohibition 'Experiment,'" 53.
33. Hamm, *Shaping the Eighteenth Amendment*, 212.
34. Warburton, *Economic Results of Prohibition*, 139.
35. Pegram, *Battling Demon Rum*, 132.
36. Ibid., 213.
37. *Baltimore Sun*, February 10–11, 1913.

38. Ibid., February 9, 1913.

39. Hamm, *Shaping the Eighteenth Amendment*, 214.

40. *Baltimore Sun*, February 10, 1913.

41. Beman, *Selected Articles*, 103.

42. Hamm, *Shaping the Eighteenth Amendment*, 212.

43. *Baltimore Sun*, February 9, 1913.

44. Ibid.

45. Ibid., February 10, 1913.

46. Ibid.

47. Cherrington, *History of the Anti-Saloon League*, 63.

48. James B. Crooks, "Maryland Progressivism," in Walsh and Fox, *Maryland*, 656.

49. Ibid., 658.

50. Ibid., 669.

51. Pickett, Wilson and Smith, *Cyclopedia of Temperance Prohibition*, 391.

52. *Baltimore Sun*, March 2, 1913.

53. Hamm, *Shaping the Eighteenth Amendment*, 235.

54. Clark, *Deliver Us from Evil*, 122.

55. Andrews, *History of Maryland*, 642.

56. Rea, "Prohibition Era in Baltimore," 27–29.

57. Ibid.

58. Odegard, *Pressure Politics*, 146.

59. Sullivan, "Supremes and Whisky by Mail," 3.

60. Ibid.

61. Ibid.

62. U.S. Supreme Court, *James Clark Distilling Company v. Western Maryland R. Co.*

63. Morone, *Hellfire Nation*, 311.

64. Rothbard, "World War One as Fulfillment," 81–125.

65. Timberlake, *Prohibition and the Progressive Movement*, 174.

66. Kobler, *Ardent Spirits*, 195.

67. The wets in Congress rallied for a six-year limit on the ratification of the amendment. See Kobler, *Ardent Spirits*, 195–99.

68. Timberlake, *Prohibition and the Progressive Movement*, 175.

69. *Baltimore Sun*, August 2, 1917; *New York Times*, August 2, 1917.

70. *New York Times*, August 4, 1917; *New York Times*, August 9, 1917.

71. Timberlake, *Prohibition and the Progressive Movement*, 174.

72. *New York Times*, December 18, 1917.

73. Ibid.

74. Ibid., December 19, 1917.

75. Kobler, *Ardent Spirits*, 198.

76. *Baltimore American*, January 23, 1918.

77. Ibid.

78. Ibid., February 4, 1918.

79. Ibid.; *Baltimore Sun*, February 8, 1918.

80. *Baltimore Sun*, February 3, 1918.

81. Ibid., February 8, 1918.

82. Ibid., February 2, 1918.

83. Ibid.

84. Ibid., February 8, 1918.

85. *Evening Sun*, February 8, 1918.

86. Ibid.

87. *Baltimore Sun*, February 9, 1918.

88. *Evening Sun*, February 8, 1918.

89. Dulaney, "Prohibition Question," 21.

90. *Evening Sun*, March 6, 1918; *Evening Sun*, March 7, 1918.

91. *Baltimore Sun*, February 14. 1918. Also see *Evening Sun*, February 9, 1918.

92. U.S. Congress, *Amendment XVIII*.

93. *Evening Sun*, April 6, 1933.

94. Ibid., December 9, 1919.

95. Ibid., July 1, 1919.

96. Ibid.

97. Ibid.

98. Ibid., July 12, 1919.

99. National Archives, *Volstead Act*.

100. Kyvig, *Repealing National Prohibition*, 13.

101. National Archives, *Volstead Act*.

102. Pegram, *Battling Demon Rum*, 150.

103. *Baltimore Sun*, October 28, 1919.

104. Ibid., October 29, 1919.

105. Pegram, *Battling Demon Rum*, 150.

106. *Baltimore American*, December 12, 1919.

107. Ibid., December 15, 1919.

108. Ibid.

109. Ibid., December 16, 1919.

110. Ibid.

111. Ibid.

112. Ibid., January 6, 1920.

113. Ibid.

114. Ibid.

115. Ibid.

116. Fitzgerald, Rabinowitch and Stites, *Russia in the Era of NEP*, 186. Also see *Evening Sun*, March 20, 1933.

117. *Baltimore Sun*, January 16, 1920.

118. Ibid.

119. Ibid.; *Evening Sun*, January 16, 1920.

120. *Evening Sun*, January 16, 1920.

121. *Baltimore Sun*, January 16, 1920.

122. *Evening Sun*, January 17, 1920.

123. *Baltimore Sun*, January 17, 1920.

124. *Evening Sun*, January 19, 1920.

125. Ibid.

126. Ibid.

127. Ibid.

128. Ibid.

129. There seemed to be a concerted effort by the ginger ale industry to supplant alcohol as the most popular beverage.

130. *Evening Sun*, January 19, 1920.

131. *New York Times*, February 25, 1920.

132. *Baltimore Sun*, February 25, 1920.

133. *New York Times*, February 25, 1920.

134. *Baltimore Sun*, February 25, 1920.

135. *New York Times*, February 26, 1920.

136. *Baltimore Sun*, March 9, 1920.

137. Ibid.

138. Ibid.

139. Ibid., March 16, 1920, and March 17, 1920.

140. Ibid., March 17, 1920.

141. Ibid., March 19, 1920.

142. Ibid., April 7, 1920.

143. Ibid.

144. Ibid.

145. Ibid.

146. Ibid.

147. *New York Times*, June 8, 1920.

148. David E. Kyvig, "National Prohibition Act (1919)," *Major Acts of Congress*, Encyclopedia.com, http://www.encyclopedia.com/history/

encyclopedias-almanacs-transcripts-and-maps/national-prohibition-act-1919.

149. Ibid.

150. Dorothy M. Brown, "Maryland Between the Wars," in Walsh and Fox, *Maryland*, 711.

Chapter 3

151. Olson, *Baltimore*, 3.

152. Odegard, *Pressure Politics*, 33.

153. Dulaney, "Prohibition Question," 64.

154. Ibid.

155. Appleby, *Positive Proof that the Bible Is Against Prohibition*.

156. Ibid.

157. For Roman Catholics in particular, this transubstantiation provides one of the key components of faith—the belief that the bread and wine became the body and blood of Jesus Christ.

158. Appleby, *Positive Proof that the Bible Is Against Prohibition*, 13–14.

159. Timberlake, *Prohibition and the Progressive Movement*, 33.

160. Ibid.

161. *New York Times*, June 7, 1926.

162. Ibid., April 26, 1930.

163. Baptist Convention of Maryland/Delaware, "Joshua Levering," http://bcmd.org/joshua-levering.

164. Ibid.

165. *Baltimore Afro-American*, April 1, 1933.

166. United Methodist Church, "Roots (1736–1816)," http://www.umc.org/who-we-are/roots.

167. *Baltimore Sun*, n.d.

168. Ibid.; December 12, 1919.

169. Hohner, *Prohibition & Politics*, 1–2.

170. Ibid., 277.

171. Pegram, "Temperance Politics and Regional Political Culture," 58.

172. *Baltimore American*, January 18, 1920.

173. *Baltimore Sun*, January 17, 1920.

174. *Baltimore American*, January 18, 1920.

175. *Baltimore Sun*, January 17, 1920.

176. Ibid.

177. *Evening Sun*, December 30, 1932.

178. Ibid., September 12, 1933.

179. Ibid.

180. *New York Times*, July 14, 1926.

181. D.G. Hart, "Machen and the OPC," http://www.opc.org/machen.html.

182. *New York Times*, February 5, 1926.

183. *Baltimore Afro-American*, April 1, 1933.

184. Ibid.

185. Ibid.

186. Ibid.

187. *New York Times*, February 27, 1922.

188. Ibid.

189. Ibid., March 6, 1922.

190. Brugger, *Maryland*, 3–5.

191. Archdiocese of Baltimore, "The Premier See (1789–1823)," https://www.archbalt.org/the-archdiocese/our-history/the-premier-see-1789-1823.

192. Odegard, *Pressure Politics*, 33.

193. Ibid., 5.

194. *Baltimore Sun*, January 17, 1920.

195. *Evening Sun*, February 7, 1918.

196. Ibid.

197. Ibid.

198. Ibid.

199. *New York Times*, February 23, 1916.

200. Ibid., January 28, 1919.

201. Ibid., December 28, 1915.

202. *Evening Sun*, February 14, 1918.

203. Foley, *Monsignor Foley on American Prohibition*, 2.

204. Ibid., 5.

205. Ibid., 3.

206. *New York Times*, April 4, 1921.

207. Brugger, *Maryland*, 453.

208. *Judiciary: Statement of Mary Haslup*, 25.

209. Gusfield, *Symbolic Crusade*, 129.

210. Jay Graybeal, "The Sandyville Loyal Temperance Legion," *Carroll County Times*, January 23, 1994.

211. Gebhart, "Movement Against Prohibition," 172.

212. *Literary Digest*, "Final Returns in 'The Digest's' Prohibition Poll," September 9, 1922, 11–13.
213. Ibid.
214. *Baltimore Sun*, September 13, 1933.
215. Mills, *Chesapeake Rum Runners of the Roaring Twenties*, 21; *Baltimore Sun*, January 17, 1920.
216. Mills, *Chesapeake Rum Runners of the Roaring Twenties*, 48–49.
217. *Baltimore Sun*, October 2, 1924.
218. *Evening Sun*, June 30, 1932.
219. Ibid.
220. Ibid., September 15, 1932.
221. *New York Times*, January 31, 1927.
222. Rose, *American Women*, 9; Pegram, *Battling Demon Rum*, 178.
223. Rose, *American Women*, 2.
224. Kyvig, "Women Against Prohibition," 473.
225. *Evening Sun*, March 10, 1933.
226. Ibid., May 12, 1933.
227. Ibid., May 18, 1933.
228. Ibid.
229. Ibid., December 14, 1932.
230. Ibid.
231. *Baltimore Sun*, October 19, 1933.
232. Olson, *Baltimore*, 83.
233. Cunz, *Maryland Germans*, 366.
234. United States Census Bureau, *Census of Population and Housing, 1920*, vol. 3, *Population, 1920*, 1,253—composition and characteristics of the population by states, https://www.census.gov/prod/www/decennial.html; Frederick N. Rasmussen, "Preserving a Part of the City's German Past," *Baltimore Sun*, January 24, 2010, www.baltimoresun.com/news/maryland/balmd.backstory24jan24,0,823486.story.
235. Cunz, *Maryland Germans*, 370.
236. Ibid.
237. Ibid., 371.
238. Ibid., 372.
239. Ibid., 496.
240. Pegram, *Battling Demon Rum*, 144.
241. Olson, *Baltimore*, 299.
242. Cunz, *Maryland Germans*, 372.
243. Olson, *Baltimore*, 345.

244. Brugger, *Maryland*, 484–85.

245. Gibbons Burke, "Henry Louis Mencken (1880–1956)," April 8, 2002, http://folk.uio.no/torgeirh/mencken/mencken_links.html.

246. Brugger, *Maryland*, 481–84.

247. *Evening Sun*, August 5, 1920.

248. Ibid., July 31, 1933.

249. Ibid., March 20, 1933.

250. Ibid.

251. Ibid.

252. Ibid., August 5, 1920.

253. Ibid., April 7, 1933; Frederick Rasmussen, "A Toast to Baltimore's Old Breweries," *Baltimore Sun*, January 1, 2012, http://articles.baltimoresun.com/2012-01-01/news/bs-md-backstory-brewery-20120101_1_first-brewery-beer-baltimore-county/2.

254. *Evening Sun*, April 10, 1933.

255. Ibid.

256. *Baltimore Sun*, October 19, 1933.

257. Ibid., September 13, 1933.

258. Ibid.

259. Ibid.

260. Walton and Taylor, "Blacks and the Southern Prohibition Movement," 247–59.

261. Ibid.

262. United States Census Bureau, "Table 21: Maryland—Race and Hispanic Origin for Selected Large Cities and Other Places: Earliest Census to 1990," http://www.census.gov/population/www/documentation/twps0076/MDtab.pdf.

263. Ibid., *Census of Population and Housing, 1920*, vol. 3.

264. Ibid. Reports by states, showing the composition and characteristics of the population for counties, cities and townships or other minor civil divisions, https://www.census.gov/prod/www/decennial.html.

265. Skotnes, "Communist Party, Anti-Racism, and the Freedom Movement."

266. Vail, "Anti-Saloon League of Maryland," 75.

267. Ibid.

268. *Christian Advocate* 88 (January 2, 1913): 23.

269. Vail, "Anti-Saloon League of Maryland," 75.

270. Turpeau, *Up from the Cane Brakes*, 40. Interestingly, Turpeau makes little reference at all in his autobiography to his work done as

department head, even misstating that he resigned from his post because the league had been successful in placing the Eighteenth Amendment in the Constitution. However, his resignation occurred in 1915. The Eighteenth Amendment did not pass Congress until 1917.

271. *Baltimore Afro-American,* January 16, 1920.

272. Ibid.

273. Sanchez, "Feminine Side of Bootlegging Louisiana History," 403–33.

274. Davis, "Race Menace in Bootlegging," 337.

275. Ibid., 342.

276. *Baltimore Afro-American*, April 1, 1933.

277. Ibid.

278. Ibid.

279. Ibid.

280. Ibid.

281. Olson, *Baltimore*, 346.

Chapter 4

282. Maryland State Board of Labor and Statistics, *Twenty-Ninth Annual Report,* 1920, http://archive.org/stream/annualreportofma1920mary/annualreportofma1920mary_djvu.txt.

283. Wheeler, "Liquor in International Trade," 145–54.

284. *New York Times*, February 13, 1905.

285. Cherrington, *History of the Anti-Saloon League*, 334.

286. *Evening Sun,* July 29, 1920.

287. Ibid.

288. Feldman, "Before and After Prohibition," 307; Gebhart, "Prohibition and Real Estate Values," 108.

289. *New York Times*, December 12, 1919.

290. Gebhart, "Prohibition and Real Estate Values," 109.

291. Kelley, *Brewing in Maryland*, 719–24.

292. Kerr, *Organized for Prohibition*, 27.

293. Ibid., 25.

294. Ibid.

295. Bready, "Maryland Rye," 346.

296. Ibid.

297. Ibid., 370.

298. *Baltimore Sun*, February 5, 1918.

299. Ibid., February 6, 1933.

300. Ibid., February 7, 1918.

301. Ibid., February 8, 1918.

302. Ibid.

303. Ibid.

304. *Evening Sun*, July 1, 1919.

305. Ibid.

306. Kelley, *Brewing in Maryland*, 142.

307. Ibid., 144–45.

308. Ibid.

309. *Baltimore Sun*, April 7, 1933.

310. David Hagberg, *J.F. Wiessner & Sons Brewing Company*, Baltimore Bottle Club, http://www.baltimorebottleclub.org/articles/wiessner.pdf.

311. Ibid.

312. *Baltimore American*, July 9, 1964.

313. Distelrath, "American Brewing Company in Baltimore, Maryland."

314. Schoeller, "American Beer on the Rocks," 24–25.

315. *Baltimore Post*, September 9, 1932.

316. German Marylanders, http://www.germanmarylanders.org/profile-index/brewers-breweries.

317. Holcomb, *City as Suburb*, 75.

318. Kelley, *Brewing in Maryland*, 579.

319. *Evening Sun*, March 17, 1933.

320. Ibid.

321. Ibid.; *Baltimore Sun*, May 29, 1939.

322. *Evening Sun*, March 24, 1933.

323. *Baltimore Sun*, April 9, 1933.

324. *Evening Sun*, March 23, 1933.

325. Ibid., April 6, 1933.

326. *Baltimore Sun*, April 7, 1933, 22.

327. Ibid.

328. Ibid.

329. Ibid.

330. Ibid., April 9, 1933.

331. Ibid.

332. *Evening Sun*, May 8, 1933.

333. Ibid., July 5, 1933.

334. Kelley, *Brewing in Maryland*, 604.

335. *New York Times*, July 17, 1933.

336. *Journal of Industrial and Engineering Chemistry*, "Alcoholic Tribulations," 591–92.

337. *New York Times*, June 11, 1921.

338. Whitaker, "Industrial Alcohol and Its Relation to Prohibition Enforcement," 647.

339. Ibid.

340. Brugger, *Maryland*, 468–69.

341. Mills, *Chesapeake Rum Runners of the Roaring Twenties*, 91.

342. Dulaney, "Prohibition Question," 36.

343. Ibid., 64.

344. Hodges, Game Apparatus Patent, April 21, 1925.

345. Morone, "Enemies of the People," 1,006.

346. Angela Dills and Jeffrey Miron, "Alcohol Prohibition and Cirrhosis" (2003), 1, http://www.nber.org/papers/w9681. Dills and Miron's data reveal that national Prohibition reduced cirrhosis by 10 to 20 percent.

347. See Blocker, "Did Prohibition Really Work?," 233–43.

348. Emerson, "Has Prohibition Promoted the Public Health?," 1,232.

349. See Angela K. Dills, Mireille Jacobson and Jeffrey A. Miron, "The Effect of Alcohol Prohibition on Alcohol Consumption: Evidence from Drunkenness Arrests," http://users.nber.org/~jacobson/Dillsetal2005.pdf; Burnham, "New Perspectives on the Prohibition 'Experiment,'" 51–68.

350. Brown, "Abstract Alcoholic Mental Disease," 175.

351. As early as 1920, there were cases of wood alcohol poisonings and deaths, even in Baltimore. *A New York Times* article from September 10, 1920, cites a particular Baltimore case in which nine civilians at the Edgewood Arsenal died as a result of drinking wood alcohol or poisoned grain alcohol. Still others suffered illness from the imbibing of alcohol that was not meant to be consumed by humans. Another example from the *New York Times*, December 8, 1927, shows that in 1927, a New York couple died as a result of drinking wood alcohol at a party held in Baltimore. These are just two examples, of many, that show that alcohol poisoning was indeed a danger during Prohibition in the 1920s.

352. O'Prey, *Brewing in Baltimore*, 61.

353. *TIME*, February 7, 1928.

354. Ibid.

355. Ibid.

356. Blum, "Chemist's War."

357. Ibid.

358. Ibid.

359. Dr. G.N. Stewart, "A Manual of Physiology with Practical Exercises," in Beman, *Selected Articles*, 12.

360. Gage, "Just What the Doctor Ordered"; Kyvig, *Repealing National Prohibition*, 30–34.

361. *TIME*, July 22, 1929.

362. Ibid.

363. Ibid.

364. The Alan Mason Chesney Medical Archives at the Johns Hopkins Medical Institutions, *A Guide to the Adolph Meyer Collection*, http://www.medicalarchives.jhmi.edu/sgml/amg-d.htm.

365. Iglehart, *King Alcohol Dethroned*, 7.

366. Adolph Meyer, "A Psychiatric Problem," in Emerson, *Alcohol and Man*, 308.

367. *TIME*, April 25, 1932.

368. *New York Times*, December 14, 1932.

369. Ibid., June 27, 1928.

370. Ibid., March 28, 1933.

371. Ibid., January 2, 1932.

372. Ibid., July 8, 1923.

373. *TIME*, August 20, 1928.

374. *New York Times*, October 14, 1928.

375. Ibid., October 28, 1928.

376. Ibid., April 12, 1931.

377. Ibid.

378. Ibid., April 15, 1931.

Chapter 5

379. Bode, *Maryland*, 174.

380. Brown, "Maryland Between the Wars," 711.

381. *TIME*, December 31, 1923.

382. Ibid.

383. *New York Times*, January 2, 1922.

384. Ibid., September 25, 1922.

385. *TIME*, October 20, 1930.

386. *New York Times*, March 17, 1922.

387. Ibid., May 7, 1922.
388. Chapelle, *Baltimore*, 190.
389. Dengler, "Training of Prohibition Enforcement Officers in the United States," 45.
390. *Time*, October 20, 1930.
391. *Evening Sun*, January 28, 1920.
392. Schmeckebier, *Bureau of Prohibition*, 67–68.
393. *New York Times*, May 5, 1923.
394. *Baltimore Sun*, January 1922.
395. *New York Times*, June 21, 1925.
396. Ibid.
397. *Evening Sun*, December 28, 1920.
398. U.S. Supreme Court, *State of Maryland v. Soper*.
399. Schmeckebier, *Bureau of Prohibition*, 172.
400. *Time*, March 25, 1929.
401. Ibid.
402. Ibid., December 1, 1930.
403. Ibid., July 7, 1930.
404. Ibid.
405. Schmeckebier, *Bureau of Prohibition*, 27.
406. U.S. Senate, "Prohibition Enforcement," 55–56, http://www.archive.org/details/prohibitionenfor00unitrich.
407. *New York Times*, August 24, 1921.
408. Ibid., March 17, 1922.
409. Lerner, *Dry Manhattan*, 261–62.
410. Ibid.
411. *Evening Sun*, January 17, 1920.
412. *New York Times*, March 19, 1920.
413. Ibid., April 3, 1920.
414. Jay A. Graybeal, "Distillery Robbed in 1923," *Carroll County Times*, November 15, 1998, http://www.hsccmd.org/Documents/Carroll%20County%20Times%20Yesteryears/1998/11-15-1998.pdf.
415. Ibid., "McGinnis Distillery Robbed Part I," *Carroll County Times*, March 8, 1998, http://www.hsccmd.org/Documents/Carroll%20County%20Times%20Yesteryears/1998/03-08-1998.pdf.
416. Ibid.
417. Ibid.
418. *New York Times*, June 1, 1920.
419. Ibid.

420. Ibid., January 9, 1921.

421. Ibid., October 20, 1921.

422. Gunter Hotel, "About Us: 100 Year Legacy," http://www.gunterhotel. net/about.

423. Ibid.

424. Maryland Historical Society Library Department, "Then and Now: The Owl Bar," in *Underbelly* (August 22, 2013), http://www.mdhs.org/ underbelly/2013/08/22/then-and-now-the-owl-bar.

425. The Owl Bar, "History," http://www.theowlbar.com/history.php.

426. Wesley Case, "Lord Baltimore Hotel to Open LB Speakeasy Bar Next Week," *Baltimore Sun*, November 30, 2016, http://www.baltimoresun. com/entertainment/music/midnight-sun-blog/bal-lord-baltimore- hotel-lb-speakeasy-opens-story.html.

427. Mills, *Chesapeake Rum Runners of the Roaring Twenties*, 23.

428. Burnham, "New Perspectives on the Prohibition 'Experiment,'" 61.

429. Gaither, *Report of the Police Commissioner*, January 3, 1933, 8.

430. *New York Times*, September 25, 1925.

431. Gaither, *Report of the Police Commissioner*.

432. Ibid.

433. Bruce, *Statement by Hon. William Cabell Bruce*.

Chapter 6

434. Tydings, *Before and After Prohibition*, 131.

435. *Time*, September 29, 1930.

436. Crooks, "Maryland Progressivism," 655.

437. *Baltimore American*, January 21, 1920.

438. William M. Bowen Jr., "The Period of Ritchie—and After," in Radoff, *Old Line State*, 128.

439. Brown, "Maryland Between the Wars," 679.

440. Andrews, *History of Maryland*, 642.

441. *New York Times*, December 18, 1922.

442. Andrews, *History of Maryland*, 642.

443. Bowen, "Period of Ritchie—and After," 129.

444. Ritchie, *Ritchie and State Prohibition Enforcement*, 3–5.

445. Ibid., *Governor Ritchie's Message*, 3–4.

446. Ibid., 4.

447. Ibid., 6.

448. Biographical Directory of the United States Congress, 1774–Present, "Bruce, William Cabell (1860–1946)," http://bioguide.congress.gov/scripts/biodisplay.pl?index=B000972.

449. *Time*, February 7, 1927.

450. Bruce, *Statement by Hon. William Cabell Bruce*.

451. Ibid.

452. Local Self Government League, *Plans to Amend National Prohibition*, 1.

453. Ibid.; *Time*, December 12, 1927.

454. Ibid.

455. Black, *Congressional Record Seventieth Congress, First Session*, 1–3.

456. *New York Times*, November 8, 1928.

457. Ibid., July 2, 1928.

458. *Baltimore Sun*, June 22, 1928.

459. Ibid., November 7, 1928.

460. Ibid., November 8, 1928.

461. *New York Times*, November 6, 1928.

462. *Baltimore Sun*, November 8, 1928.

463. Ibid.

464. Biographical Directory, "Bruce, William Cabell."

465. *Baltimore Sun*, September 13, 1933.

466. Ibid.

467. Arlington National Cemetery, "John Boynton Philip Clayton Hill Lieutenant Colonel, United States Army Member of Congress," November 2000, http://www.arlingtoncemetery.com/jbhill.htm.

468. Ibid.; *New York Times*, November 15, 1922; Johnson et al., *Sun Papers of Baltimore*, 396.

469. Johnson et al., *Sun Papers of Baltimore*, 395.

470. Ibid.

471. Ibid., 396.

472. *Time*, November 24, 1924.

473. Brugger, *Maryland*, 470.

474. Ibid.

475. Johnson et al., *Sun Papers of Baltimore*, 396.

476. *New York Times*, February 22, 1922.

477. Ibid., April 27, 1921.

478. Ibid., September 28, 1923.

479. Ibid., September 19, 1924.

480. Ibid.

481. *Time*, November 24, 1924.

482. Ibid.
483. Biographical Directory of the United States Congress, 1774–Present, "Hill, John Boynton Philip Clayton (1879–1941)," http://bioguide. congress.gov/scripts/biodisplay.pl?index=H000597.
484. *Evening Sun*, March 23, 1933.
485. Ibid., October 18, 1933.
486. Ibid.
487. Chapelle, *Baltimore*, 190.
488. *New York Times*, June 29, 1932.
489. Argersinger, *Toward a New Deal in Baltimore*, 16–17.
490. *New York Times*, January 2, 1914.
491. Okrent, *Last Call*, 233.
492. Ibid., 295.
493. Ibid., 233; Levine, "Standing Political Decisions and Critical Realignment," 3.
494. *Evening Sun*, December 16, 1920.
495. *Baltimore Magazine*, "Classified Ad" (June 1927): 26, http://external. bcpl.lib.md.us/hcdo/baltmag/pdf/b1927/06/b2706026.pdf.
496. *Time*, September 17, 1928.
497. *New York Times*, November 10, 1922.
498. Ibid., November 15, 1922.
499. *Time*, May 19, 1930.
500. Ibid., May 7, 1928.
501. Okrent, *Last Call*, 333.
502. Ibid., 332–33.
503. *Baltimore Sun*, November 8, 1928.
504. Lichtman, *Prejudice and the Old Politics*, 85.
505. Parsley, "Presidential Politics," 69–70.
506. Ibid., 69.
507. *New York Times*, October 30, 1928.
508. Ibid.
509. Ibid.
510. Dave Leip, "1928 Presidential General Election Results," Atlas of U.S. Presidential Elections, http://uselectionatlas.org/RESULTS/index. html.
511. Levine, "Standing Political Decisions and Critical Realignment," 313.
512. Ibid.
513. Lichtman, *Prejudice and the Old Politics*, 77.
514. Ibid., 92.

515. Ibid., 243.

516. Parsley, "Presidential Politics," 83.

517. *Evening Sun*, November 6, 1930.

518. Ibid.

519. Ibid., November 8, 1930.

520. Ibid., November 6, 1930.

521. Hoover, *Memoirs of Herbert Hoover: The Cabinet and the Presidency*, 201–2.

522. Kyvig, *Repealing National Prohibition*, 99–100.

523. Ritchie, *Electing FDR*, 52.

524. Kyvig, "Raskob, Roosevelt, and Repeal," 469.

525. Oulahan, *The Man Who…*, 102.

526. *Evening Sun*, June 30, 1932.

527. Oulahan, *The Man Who…*, 102.

528. Bowen, "Period of Ritchie—and After," 696.

529. Roosevelt, *Public Papers and Addresses of Franklin D. Roosevelt*, vol. 1, 70–71.

530. *New York Times*, October 26, 1926.

531. Ibid.

532. Ibid.

533. Franklin D. Roosevelt, "Roosevelt Campaign Address at Baltimore, MD," in *Public Papers and Addresses of Franklin D. Roosevelt*, vol. 1, 839.

534. Ibid.

535. Ibid.

536. Ibid.

537. *New York Times*, October 26, 1932.

538. Ibid.

539. Pegram, *Battling Demon Rum*, 185.

540. U.S. Senate, "Party Division in the Senate, 1789–Present," http://www.senate.gov/pagelayout/history/one_item_and_teasers/partydiv.htm; Office of the Clerk, House of Representatives, "House History: 73rd Congress (1933–1935)," http://artandhistory.house.gov/house_history/index.aspx?cong=73.

541. *Evening Sun*, November 9, 1932.

542. Maryland State Archives, *Maryland Manual*, vol. 150, 269–73, http://msa.maryland.gov/megafile/msa/speccol/sc2900/sc2908/000001/000150/html/am150--269.html.

543. Bowen, "Period of Ritchie—and After," 697.

544. Parsley, "Presidential Politics," 137.

545. *Evening Sun*, November 9, 1932.

546. Ibid.

547. Ibid.

548. Ibid.

549. Parsley, "Presidential Politics," 100.

550. Ibid.

551. Levine, "Standing Political Decisions and Critical Realignment," 319.

552. Kennedy, *Freedom from Fear*, 32; Lichtman, *Prejudice and the Old Politics*, argues that the Depression had truly been the catalyst of change in realigning America's voting and political behavior.

Chapter 7

553. *TIME*, February 27, 1933.

554. U.S. Congress, *Twenty First Amendment—Repeal of the 18th Amendment*, Find Law, http://caselaw.lp.findlaw.com/data/constitution/amendment21.

555. Ibid.; *New York Times*, April 16, 1932.

556. *Evening Sun*, February 20, 1933; U.S. Congress, *Twenty First Amendment*.

557. Pare Lorentz Center at the FDR Presidential Library, "Franklin D. Roosevelt; Day by Day," http://www.fdrlibrary.marist.edu/daybyday/resource/march-1933-6.

558. Baltimore City Liquor License Board, http://llb.baltimorecity.gov.

559. *Baltimore Sun*, April 5, 1933.

560. Ibid., April 6, 1933.

561. Ibid.

562. Ibid.

563. Ibid.

564. *Evening Sun*, April 7, 1933.

565. Ibid.

566. Ibid., March 20, 1933.

567. Ibid., July 5, 1933.

568. *Baltimore Afro-American*, April 8, 1933.

569. Ibid.

570. *Evening Sun*, April 6, 1933.

571. Ibid.

572. *Baltimore Sun*, April 8, 1933.

573. *Evening Sun*, March 23, 1933.

574. Ibid., April 6, 1933.

575. Ibid., March 23, 1933.

576. Ibid., April 5, 1933,

577. *Baltimore Sun*, April 8, 1933.

578. Tom Chalkley, "Wet Stone," *Baltimore City Paper*, April 2–8, 2003.

579. Ibid.

580. *Baltimore Sun*, April 7, 1933.

581. *Evening Sun*, April 7, 1933.

582. *Baltimore Sun*, April 7, 1933.

583. Ibid.

584. Ibid., April 8, 1933.

585. *Evening Sun*, April 7, 1933.

586. *Baltimore Sun*, April 8, 1933.

587. *Evening Sun*, April 7, 1933.

588. Ibid., April 8, 1933.

589. Ibid., April 10, 1933.

590. Ibid., May 8, 1933.

591. *Catonsville Herald and Baltimore Countian*, April 28, 1933.

592. Ibid.

593. Ibid., May 5, 1933.

594. Richard M. Evans, "The VCL: Architects of Repeal," http://www.druglibrary.org/schaffer/alcohol/vcl1.htm.

595. Schaller, "Democracy at Rest," 82–85.

596. Maryland State Archives, *Maryland Manual*, vol. 421, 447, http://msa.maryland.gov/megafile/msa/speccol/sc2900/sc2908/000001/000421/html/am421--447.html.

597. Ibid.

598. *Evening Sun*, September 12, 1933.

599. *Baltimore Sun*, September 12, 1933.

600. *New York Times*, November 8, 1933; Schaller, "Democracy at Rest," 89.

601. *Evening Sun*, September 13, 1933.

602. *Baltimore Sun*, September 13, 1933.

603. Ibid.

604. *Evening Sun*, September 13, 1933.

605. *Baltimore Sun*, September 13, 1933.

606. *Evening Sun*, September 13, 1933.

607. Maryland State Archives, *Maryland Manual*, vol. 150, 292, http://www.mdarchives.state.md.us/megafile/msa/speccol/sc2900/sc2908/000001/000150/html/am150—292.html?.

608. Ibid.; *Baltimore Sun*, September 13, 1933.

609. *Evening Sun*, September 12, 1933.

610. *Baltimore Sun*, September 13, 1933.

611. Ibid.

612. Ethan P. Davis, "Liquor Laws and Constitutional Conventions: A Legal History of the Twenty-first Amendment," Yale Law School: Student Scholarship Papers, April 9, 2008, http://digitalcommons.law.yale.edu/cgi/viewcontent.cgi?article=1065&context=student_papers&sei-redir=1#search=%22Ethan%20Davis%20%2B%20Prohibition%22.

613. Schaller, "Democracy at Rest," 87.

614. *Baltimore Sun*, September 13, 1933.

615. *New York Times*, September 13, 1933.

616. *Baltimore Sun*, September 13, 1933; *Evening Sun*, October 18, 1933.

617. Brown, *Ratification of the 21ˢᵗ Amendment*, 191.

618. Ibid., 200–201.

619. Ibid., 202.

620. *Evening Sun*, October 18, 1933.

621. Ibid., August 11, 1933.

622. Ibid., December 14, 1933.

623. Ibid., September 13, 1933.

624. Franklin D. Roosevelt, "Date of Repeal of the Eighteenth Amendment," National Archives and Records Administration, https://www.archives.gov/files/historical-docs/doc-content/images/21st-amendment-fdr-proclamation.pdf.

625. Ibid., "Proclamation 2065—Repeal of the Eighteenth Amendment, December 5, 1933," American Presidency Project, http://www.presidency.ucsb.edu/ws/index.php?pid=14570.

626. Ibid.

627. Ibid.

628. *Evening Sun*, December 6, 1933.

629. Ibid.

630. *Catonsville Herald and Baltimore Countian*, December 22, 1933.

631. *Evening Sun*, December 5, 1933.

632. Ibid.

633. Ibid.

634. Ibid.

635. Ibid., December 4, 1933.

636. Ibid., December 5, 1933.

637. Ibid.

638. Ibid., December 4, 1933.

639. *Catonsville Herald and Baltimore Countian*, January 5, 1934.

640. Ibid.

641. Cyril Penn, "Is Prohibition Alive and Well in America," *Wine Business Monthly* (March 2005).

642. Sarah Gantz, "Sagamore Spirit Debuts Its Port Covington Distillery," *Baltimore Sun*, April 20, 2017, http://www.baltimoresun.com/business/bs-bz-sagamore-spirit-distillery-20170420-story.html. Please also see the latest revival of "heritage" Maryland rye whiskeys—including Melvale Rye, Melky Miller 8-Year-Old American Whiskey, Maryland Pure Rye Club Whiskey—by New Liberty Distiller (located in Philadelphia, Pennsylvania). Its website is located at https://newlibertydistillery.com/spirits/heritage/melvale.

643. Havre de Grace is a relatively small town in Harford County that is situated along the banks of the Susquehanna River at the head of the Chesapeake Bay. The town thus provided prime waterways for rumrunners and bootleggers from the top of the Chesapeake on down and between its many tributaries. Havre de Grace was often called "Little Chicago" by its residents and by Marylanders alike for its notoriety of attracting gamblers, bookies and gangsters, among others, who liked to visit and presumably do business at the town's racetrack. An episode of the popular Prohibition-themed HBO program *Boardwalk Empire* even had an episode titled "Havre de Grace" in 2013.

644. Christiana Amarachi Mbakwe, "Havre de Grace Speakeasy Museum Documents the Resistance to Prohibition," *Baltimore Sun*, August 19, 2016, http://www.baltimoresun.com/news/maryland/harford/harford-magazine/ph-mg-ha-history-of-resistance-havre-de-grace-20160816-story.html.

645. Rick Hampson, "Dry America's Not-So-Sober Reality: It's Shrinking Fast," *USA Today*, http://www.usatoday.com/news/nation/2010-06-30-dry-counties_N.htm.

646. Susan Singer-Bart, "Damascus Is Still a Dry Town, and Likely to Stay that Way," Gazette.net, June 14, 2000, http://ww2.gazette.net/gazette_archive/2000/200024/germantown/news/14995-1.html.

647. Steve Hendrix, "In Montgomery, Dry Damascus Prepares to Embrace Beer and Wine," *Washington Post*, January 6, 2013, https://www.washingtonpost.com/local/in-montgomery-dry-damascus-prepares-to-embrace-beer-and-wine/2013/01/06/a362a1ac-447e-11e2-8e70-e1993528222d_story.html?utm_term=.a0c9747011c1.

648. U.S. Supreme Court, *Granholm, Governor of Michigan, et al. v, Heald et al.*

SELECTED BIBLIOGRAPHY

This selected bibliography contains essential primary and secondary sources related to Prohibition and Maryland history that were consulted for this work. Additional sources are also cited in "Notes."

Primary Sources

Alcohol, Hygiene and the Public Schools: Digest of State Laws. Department of Justice, Washington, D.C. Published by the Division of Research and Public Information, Bureau of Prohibition. Washington, D.C.: Government Printing Offce, 1931.

Andrews, Lincoln C. "Prohibition Enforcement as a Phase of Federal versus State Jurisdiction in American Life." *Annals of the American Academy of Political and Social Science* 129 (January 1927): 77–87.

Appleby, Samuel C. *Positive Proof that the Bible Is Against Prohibition*. Baltimore, MD: Torch Publishing Company, 1920.

Association Against the Prohibition Amendment. *Association Against the Prohibition Amendment Maryland Division Newsletter*, July 5, 1929. Record located at Maryland State Archives, Governor (General File) MSA no. S 1041-471.

Baltimore Afro-American. 1920–33.

Baltimore American. 1919–20.

Baltimore Evening Sun. 1913–33.

Baltimore Sun. 1913–33.

Battaglia, Joseph. "Letter to Governor Ritchie from Joseph Battaglia." January 6, 1930. Record located at Maryland State Archives, Governor (General File) MSA no. S 1041-471.

Beman, Lamar T. *Selected Articles on the Prohibition of the Liquor Traffic.* White Plains, NY: H.W. Wilson Company, 1915.

Black, Hugo L. *The Congressional Record Seventieth Congress, First Session Speech of Hon. Hugo L. Black of Ala. in Reply to William Cabell Bruce, of MD in the Senate of the United States Tuesday May 15, 1928.* United States: [self-published?], 1928.

Borah, William E. "The Eighteenth Amendment: A Greater Question than the Liquor Question Is the Capacity of the American People for Constitutional Government: Speech of William E. Borah Delivered before the Presbyterian General Assembly at Baltimore, MD May 30, 1926." Washington, D.C.: Government Printing Office, 1926.

Brown, Everett Somerville. *Ratification of the 21st Amendment to the Constitution of the US: State Convention Records and Laws.* Reprint, New York: Law Book Exchange Ltd., 2003. Originally published by University of Michigan Press, 1938.

Bruce, William Cabell. "Is Prohibition a Success After Five Years? No!" August 1925. Record located at Maryland State Archives, Governor (General File) MSA no. S 1041-471.

———. *Statement by Hon. William Cabell Bruce.* In *The National Prohibition Law: Hearings before the Subcommittee of the Committee on the Judiciary United States Senate—Sixty-Ninth Congress.* http://www.druglibrary.org/schaffer/history/e1920/senj1926/cabellbruce.htm.

———. "Three Addresses on Prohibition." 1925. Record located at Maryland State Archives, Governor (General File) MSA no. S 1041-471.

Catonsville Herald and Baltimore Countian. 1933.

Cherrington, Ernest H. *The History of the Anti-Saloon League.* Westerville, OH: American Issue Publishing Company, 1913.

Congressional Record 68th Congress, First Session. "Speech of John Philip Hill of MD in House." April 9, 1824. Record located at Maryland State Archives, Governor (General File) MSA no. S 1041-470. Department of Justice (General Records, Record Group 60 1790–1989, 1991). *60.15.4 Records of the Bureau of Prohibition.* https://www.archives.gov/research/guide-fed-records/groups/060.html#60.15.4.

Dulaney, Harry S. "The Prohibition Question Viewed from the Economic and Moral Standpoint." *Manufacturer's Record.* Baltimore, MD: Manufacturer's Record Publishing Company, 1922.

Emerson, Haven. "Has Prohibition Promoted the Public Health?" *American Journal of Public Health* 12 (December 17, 1927): 1,230–34.

Feldman, Herman. "Before and After Prohibition." *Journal of the American Statistical Association* 25, no. 172 (December 1930): 497–98.

Foley, Monsignor. *Monsignor Foley on American Prohibition.* Westerville: American Issue Publishing Company, 1930.

The Foundation, Progress, and Principles of the Washington Temperance Society of Baltimore and the Influence It Has Had on the Temperance Movements in the United States. Baltimore, MD: John D. Troy, 1842.

Franklin, Fabian. *What Prohibition Has Done to America.* New York: Harcourt, Brace & Company, 1922.

Gaither, Charles D. *Report of the Police Commissioner for the City of Baltimore,* 1917–34. Records at Enoch Pratt Central Library, Baltimore, Maryland.

———. "Report to His Excellency, the Governor of Maryland, Annapolis, Maryland." *Board of Police Commissioners Report: 1934.* Baltimore, Maryland, 1935, 535.

———. "Report to His Excellency, the Governor of Maryland, Annapolis, Maryland." *Board of Police Commissioners Report: 1932.* Baltimore, Maryland, 1933.

Gebhart, John C. "Movement Against Prohibition." *Annals of the American Academy of Political and Social Science.* Vol. 163, *Prohibition: A National Experiment* (September 1932): 172–80.

———. "Prohibition and Real Estate Values." *Annals of the American Academy of Political and Social Science.* Vol. 163, *Prohibition: A National Experiment* (September 1932): 105–12.

Gordon, Ernest B. *The Maine Law.* New York: Fleming H. Revell Company, 1919.

Higgins, Edwin. *Prohibition for Maryland: Published by Order of the Executive Committee of the Maryland State Temperance Alliance.* Baltimore, MD: D.H. Carroll, 1886.

Hill, John Philip. "Hill to Ritchie on Prohibition." September 28, 1923. Record located at Maryland State Archive, Governor (General File) MSA no. S 1041-471.

Hodges, Arthur. Game Apparatus Patent, April 21, 1925. http://www.google.com/patents/about/1534591_GAME_APPARATUS.html?id=5qZqAAAAEBAJ.

Hoover, Herbert. *The Memoirs of Herbert Hoover: The Cabinet and the Presidency, 1920–1933.* New York, 1952.

————. *The Memoirs of Herbert Hoover: The Great Depression, 1929–1941*. New York, 1952.

Iglehart, Ferdinand. *King Alcohol Dethroned*. Westerville: American Issue Publishing Company, 1919.

Jackson, J.C. "The Work of the Anti-Saloon League." *Annals of the American Academy of Political and Social Science*. Vol. 32, *Regulation of the Liquor Traffic* (November 1908): 12–26.

Journal of Industrial and Engineering Chemistry. "Alcoholic Tribulations" (July 1921): 591–92.

Judiciary: Statement of Mary Haslup, Amendment Prohibiting Intoxicating Liquors. Washington, D.C.: Government Printing Office, 1914.

Kach, Paul R. "Another Thought on Prohibition Enforcement." *Virginia Law Register* 11, no. 11, New Series (March 1926): 655–61.

Levering, Joshua. "Prohibition: Whence Came It and Why?: An Address Delivered in the University Baptist Church, Baltimore, Md., November 21st, 1930." Baltimore, Maryland, 1930.

Literary Digest. August–September 1922.

Local Self Government League. *Plans to Amend National Prohibition without Repealing Either the Eighteenth Amendment of the Volstead Act; Also to Divorce Prohibition from Politics*. Baltimore, MD: Chamber of Commerce, 1931.

Manufacturer's Record. "Prohibition Has Justified Itself as Judged by Many of the Foremost Business Men and Educators of the Country." Baltimore, MD: Manufacturer's Record Publishing Company, 1925.

Marbury, William L. *Address of William L. Marbury on National Prohibition before the Federal Relations Committee of the Maryland Legislature*. New York: H.W. Wilson Company, 1918.

National Archives. *The Volstead Act 10/28/1919*. https://www.docsteach. org/documents/document/volstead-act.

National Commission on Law Observance and Enforcement. *Report on the Enforcement of the Prohibition Laws of the United States* (Wickersham Commission Report on Alcohol Prohibition), January 7, 1931. Online Library of Drug Policy. http://www.druglibrary.org/schaffer/library/studies/wick/index.html.

New York Times. 1913–33.

Poe, Edgar Allan. *Judge Clark's Decision of the Constitutionality of the 18th Amendment before the Supreme Court on Appeal*. Baltimore, MD: The Crusaders, 1931.

Ritchie, Albert C. *Beer and Liquor Control in Maryland*. Baltimore, MD, 1933.

————. *Governor (General File) Prohibition and Repeal 1920-1935*. Records at Maryland State Archives, MSA nos. S 1041-470 and S 1041-473.

———. *Governor Ritchie's Message to the Extraordinary Session of the General Assembly of Maryland, November 23, 1933*. Baltimore, MD, 1933.

———. *Ritchie and State Prohibition Enforcement*. Baltimore, MD: Ritchie Citizenship League, 1932.

Rogers, Lindsay. "The Constitutionality of the Webb-Kenyon Bill." *California Law Review* 1, no. 6 (September 1913): 499–512.

Roosevelt, Franklin D. *The Public Papers and Addresses of Franklin D. Roosevelt*. Vol. 1, *The Genesis of the New Deal, 1928–1932*. New York, 1938.

Schmeckebier, Laurence F. *The Bureau of Prohibition: Its History, Activities, and Organization*. Washington, D.C.: Brookings Institute, 1929.

Sunderland, Edson. "Preliminary Report on Observance and Enforcement of Prohibition and the Report Supplemental Thereto: Comment." *Michigan Law Review* 30, no. 1 (November 1931): 4–6.

TIME magazine. 1923–33.

Tydings, Millard E. *Before and After Prohibition*. New York: MacMillan Company, 1930.

U.S. Congress. *Amendment XVIII*. National Archives. https://www.archives.gov/founding-docs/amendments-11-27.

———. *Amendment XXI*. FindLaw. http://caselaw.lp.findlaw.com/data/constitution/amendment21.

U.S. House of Representatives. "Repeal of Wartime Prohibition." Hearings before the Committee on Agriculture, Sixty-Sixth Congress, Second Session, December 9 and 13, 1919.

U.S. Senate. "Prohibition Enforcement. Letter from the Secretary of the Treasury." Document no. 198, Sixty-Ninth Congress, Second Session, 1927.

U.S. Supreme Court. *Granholm, Governor of Michigan, et al. v, Heald et al. Certiorari to the United States Court of Appeals for the Sixth Circuit No. 03-1116, Argued December 7, 2004–Decided May 16, 2005*. https://www.law.cornell.edu/supct/html/03-1116.ZS.html.

———. *James Clark Distilling Company v. Western Maryland R. Co.* 242 U.S. 311 (1917). http://caselaw.lp.findlaw.com/cgi-bin/getcase.pl?court=us&vol=242&invol=311.

———. *Mugler v. Kansas*. No. 152, 1887. http://caselaw.findlaw.com/us-supreme-court/123/623.html.

———. *State of Maryland v. Soper*. 270 U.S. 9 (1926). http://caselaw.lp.findlaw.com/cgibin/getcase.pl?friend=o&navby=volpage&court=us&vol=270&page=22.

"Webb-Kenyon Act (1913)." In Fosdick, Raymond, and Albert Scott. *Toward Liquor Control*. New York, 1933.

Wheeler, Wayne B. "Liquor in International Trade." *Annals of the American Academy of Political and Social Science.* Vol. 109, *Prohibition and Its Enforcement* (September 1923): 145–54.

Willcox, Walter F. "An Attempt to Measure Public Opinion About Repealing the Eighteenth Amendment." *Journal of the American Statistical Association* 26, no. 175 (September 1931): 243–61.

Windle, Charles A. "C.A Windle, Editor, the Iconoclast, Answers Billy Sunday's 'Booze' Sermon: Address Delivered at Maryland Theatre, Baltimore, Md., Sunday, March 19, 1916: under Auspices Personal Liberty League of Maryland." Baltimore, MD: Allied Printing Trades Council, 1916.

Secondary Sources

Alexander, Ruth M. "'We Are Engaged as a Band of Sisters': Class and Domesticity in the Washington Temperance Movement, 1840–1850." *Journal of American History* 75, no. 3 (December 1988): 763–85.

Allsop, Kenneth. *Bootleggers: The Story of Chicago's Prohibition Era.* London: Hutchinson, 1968.

Anderson, Lloyd. "Direct Shipment of Wine, the Commerce Clause, and the Twenty-First Amendment: A Call for Legislative Reform." *Akron Law Review* (July 2015). http://ideaexchange.uakron.edu/cgi/viewcontent.cgi?article=1343&context=akronlawreview.

Andrews, Matthew Page. *History of Maryland: Province and State.* Hatboro, PA: Tradition Press, 1965.

Argersinger, Jo Anne. *Toward a New Deal in Baltimore: People and Government in the Great Depression.* Chapel Hill: University of North Carolina Press, 1988.

Arnold, Joseph L., and Anirban Basu. *Maryland: Old Line to New Prosperity.* Northridge, CA: Windsor Publications, 1985.

Bader, Robert Smith. *Prohibition in Kansas: A History.* Lawrence: University Press of Kansas, 1986.

Behr, Edward. *Prohibition: Thirteen Years that Changed America.* New York: Arcade Publishing, 1996.

Beman, Lamar T. *Selected Articles on Prohibition: Modification of the Volstead Law.* New York, 1924.

Blocker, Jack S., Jr. *American Temperance Movements: Cycles of Reform.* Boston: Twayne Publishers, 1989.

———. "Did Prohibition Really Work?: Alcohol Prohibition as a Public Health Innovation." *American Journal of Public Health* 96, no. 2 (February 2006): 233–43.

———. *Retreat from Reform: The Prohibition Movement in the United States, 1890–1913.* Westport, CT: Greenwood Press, 1976.

Blum, Deborah. "The Chemist's War." *Slate*, September 20, 2011. http:// www.slate.com/id/2245188.

———. *The Poisoner's Handbook: Murder and the Birth of Forensic Medicine in Jazz Age New York.* New York: Penguin Press, 2010.

Bode, Carl. *Maryland: A Bicentennial History.* Nashville, TN: W.W. Norton & Company Inc., 1978.

Bready, James H. "Maryland Rye: A Whiskey the Nation Long Fancied— but Now Has Let Vanish." *Maryland Historical Magazine* (Winter 1990): 346.

Brown, Frederick. "Abstract Alcoholic Mental Disease Before and After Prohibition," *Journal of the American Statistical Association* (March 1932): 175.

Brugger, Robert J. *Maryland: A Middle Temperament, 1634–1980.* Baltimore: Johns Hopkins University Press, in association with the Maryland Historical Society, 1988.

Burner, David. *The Politics of Provincialism: The Democratic Party in Transition, 1918–1932.* New York: W.W. Norton & Company, 1967.

Burnham, John C. "New Perspectives on the Prohibition 'Experiment' of the 1920s." *Journal of Social History* 2 (1968): 51–68.

Byse, Clark. "Alcoholic Beverage Control before Repeal." *Law and Contemporary Problems* 7, no. 4 (Autumn 1940): 544–69.

Chapelle, Suzanne Ellery Greene. *Baltimore: An Illustrated History.* Sun Valley, CA: American Historical Press, 2000.

Clark, Norman H. *Deliver Us from Evil: An Interpretation of American Prohibition.* New York: W.W. Norton and Company Inc., 1976.

Crooks, James B. *Politics & Progress: The Rise of Urban Progressivism in Baltimore, 1895 to 1911.* Baton Rouge: Louisiana State University Press, 1968.

Cunz, Dieter. *The Maryland Germans: A History.* Princeton, NJ: Princeton University Press, 1948.

Davis, Charles Hall. "The Race Menace in Bootlegging." *Virginia Law Register* 7, no. 5, New Series (September 1921): 337.

Dengler, Harry M. "Training of Prohibition Enforcement Officers in the United States." *American Journal of Police Science* 2, no. 1 (January–February 1931): 45.

Dills, Angela. "Intended and Unintended Consequences of Policies: Essays on Test Scores and House Prices, Peer Effects and Alcohol Prohibition." PhD diss., Boston University, 2003.

Distelrath, Art. "The American Brewing Company in Baltimore, Maryland." *American Breweriana Journal*, no. 105 (July–August 2000). https://americanbreweriana.org/magazine/issues/issues_detail.php?selectid=105.

Dobyns, Fletcher. *The Amazing Story of Repeal: An Expose of the Power of Propaganda.* Chicago: Willett, Clark & Company, 1940.

Emerson, Haven. *Alcohol and Man.* New York: Arno Press, 1981.

Fitzgerald, Sheila, Alexander Rabinowitch and Richard Stites. *Russia in the Era of NEP.* Bloomington: Indiana University Press, 1991.

Ford, Everett J., and Janice E. Ford. *Pre-Prohibition Beer Bottles and Breweries of Baltimore, MD.* Baltimore, MD: Ford Publishing, 1974.

Fosdick, Raymond B., and Albert L. Scott. *Toward Liquor Control.* New York, 1933.

Gage, Beverly. "Just What the Doctor Ordered." *Smithsonian Magazine* (April 2005). http://www.smithsonianmag.com/historyarchaeology/Just_What_the_Doctor_Ordered.htm.

Graebner, William. "Federalism in the Progressive Era: A Structural Interpretation of Reform." *Journal of American History* 64 (September 1977): 331–57.

Gusfield, Joseph R. *Symbolic Crusade: Status Politics and the American Temperance Movement.* Urbana: University of Illinois Press, 1963.

Habicht, Frederick. "Ratification of the 18th Amendment by the MD Legislature as a Rural Urban Issue." Master's thesis, Morgan State University, 1968.

Hamm, Richard F. *Shaping the Eighteenth Amendment: Temperance Reform, Legal Culture, and the Polity, 1880–1920.* Chapel Hill: University of North Carolina Press, 1995.

Harrison, S.L. *The Editorial Art of Edmund Duffy.* 1st ed. Madison, NJ: Fairleigh Dickinson University Press, 1998.

Hawley, Ellis W. *The Great War and the Search for a Modern Order: A History of the American People and Their Institutions, 1917–1933.* 2nd ed. Prospect Heights, IL: Waveland Press, 1992.

Hohner, Robert A. "Bishop Cannon's Apprenticeship in Temperance Politics, 1901–1918." *Journal of Southern History* 34, no. 1 (February 1968): 33–49.

———. *Prohibition & Politics: The Life of Bishop James Cannon, Jr.* Columbia: University of South Carolina Press, 1999.

Holcomb, Eric L. *The City as Suburb: A History of Northeast Baltimore Since 1660.* Chicago: Center for American Places, 2008.

Johns, Bud. *The Ombibulous Mr. Mencken.* San Francisco: Synergistic Press, 1968.

Johnson, Gerald, Frank R. Kent, H.L. Mencken and Hamilton Owens. *The Sun Papers of Baltimore.* New York: Alfred A. Knopf, 1937.

Jones, John C. "Prohibition in the Free State." Honors Paper, no. 52, Department of History, U.S. Naval Academy, Annapolis, Maryland, 1991.

Karl, Barry D. *The Uneasy State: The United States from 1915 to 1945.* Chicago: University of Chicago Press, 1991.

Kasper, Rob. *Baltimore Beer: A Satisfying History of Charm City Brewing.* Charleston, SC: The History Press, 2011.

Kavieff, Paul. *The Violent Years: Prohibition and the Detroit Mobs.* Fort Lee, NJ: Barricade Books, 2001.

Kelley, William J. *Brewing in Maryland.* Baltimore, MD: Kelly Publishing, 1965.

Kennedy, David M. *Freedom from Fear: The American People in Depression and War, 1929–1945.* New York: Oxford University Press, 1999.

Kerr, K. Austin. *Organized for Prohibition: A New History of the Anti-Saloon League.* New Haven: Yale University Press, 1985.

Kingdon, John W. *Agendas, Alternatives, and Public Policies.* New York: Longman, 2003.

Kobler, John. *Ardent Spirits: The Rise and Fall of Prohibition.* New York: Putnam, 1973.

Kyvig, David. "Raskob, Roosevelt, and Repeal." *Historian* 37, no. 3 (May 1975): 469–87.

Kyvig, David E. *Repealing National Prohibition.* Chicago: University of Chicago Press, 1979.

———. "Women Against Prohibition." *American Quarterly* 28, no. 4 (Autumn 1976): 465–82.

Lerner, Michael A. *Dry Manhattan: Prohibition in New York City.* Cambridge, MA: Harvard University Press, 2007.

Leuchtenberg, William E. *The Perils of Prosperity, 1914–1932.* Chicago, 1993.

Levine, Marc V. "Standing Political Decisions and Critical Realignment: The Pattern of American Politics, 1872–1948." *Journal of Politics* 38, no. 2 (May 1976): 292–25.

Lichtman, Allan J. "Critical Election Theory and the Reality of American Presidential Politics, 1916–40." *American Historical Review* 81, no. 2 (April 1976): 317–51.

————. *Prejudice and the Old Politics: The Presidential Election of 1928*. Chapel Hill, NC, 1979.

Link, Arthur S., and Richard L. McCormick. *Progressivism*. Wheeling, IL: Harlan Davidson Inc., 1983.

Mason, Philip P. *Rumrunning and the Roaring Twenties: Prohibition on the Michigan-Ontario Waterway*. Detroit, MI: Wayne State University Press, 1995.

Mills, Eric. *Chesapeake Rum Runners of the Roaring Twenties*. Centreville, VA: Tidewater Publishers, 2000.

Moore, Mark H., and Dean R. Gerstein, eds. *Alcohol and Public Policy: Beyond the Shadow of Prohibition*. Washington, D.C.: National Academy Press, 1981.

Morone, James. "Enemies of the People: The Moral Dimensions of Public Health." *Journal of Health Politics, Policy, and Law* 22, no. 4 (1997): 1,006.

————. *Hellfire Nation: The Politics of Sin in American History*. New Haven, CT: Yale University Press, 2003.

Munger, Michael, and Thomas Schaller. "The Prohibition Amendments: A Natural Experiment in Interest Group Influence." *Public Choice* 90 (1997): 139–63.

Murphy, Mary. "Bootlegging Mothers and Drinking Daughters: Gender and Prohibition in Butte, Montana." *American Quarterly* 46, no. 2 (1994): 174–94.

Neumann, Caryn E. "The End of Gender Solidarity: The History of the Women's Organization for National Prohibition Reform in the United States, 1929–1933." *Journal of Women's History* 9, no. 2 (Summer 1997): 31–51.

Odegard, Peter H. *Pressure Politics: The Story of the Anti-Saloon League*. New York: Octagon Books Inc., 1966.

Okrent, Daniel. *Last Call: The Rise and Fall of Prohibition*. New York: Scribner, 2010.

Olson, Sherry H. *Baltimore: The Building of an American City*. Baltimore, MD: Johns Hopkins University Press, 1996.

O'Prey, Maureen. *Brewing in Baltimore*. Charleston, SC: Arcadia Publishing, 2012.

Oulahan, Richard. *The Man Who…: The Story of the 1932 Democratic National Convention*. New York, 1971.

Parsley, Shannon Lee. "Presidential Politics and the Building of the Roosevelt Coalition in Baltimore City, 1924–1936." Master's thesis, University of Maryland, May 2001.

Peck, Garrett. *Prohibition in Washington, D.C.: How Dry We Weren't*. Charleston, SC: The History Press, 2011.

Pegram, Thomas R. *Battling Demon Rum: The Struggle for a Dry America, 1800–1933*. Chicago: Ivan R. Dee, 1998.

———. "Hoodwinked: The Anti-Saloon League and the Ku Klux Klan in the 1920s Prohibition Enforcement." *Journal of Gilded Age and Progressive Era* 7, no. 1 (2008).

———. "Kluxing the Eighteenth Amendment: The Anti-Saloon League, the Ku Klux Klan, and the Fate of Prohibition in the 1920s." In *American Public Life and the Historical Imagination*. Edited by Wendy Gamber, Michael Grossberg and Hendrik Hartog. South Bend, IN: University of Notre Dame Press, 2003, 240–61.

———. "Prohibition." In *The American Congress: The Building of Democracy*. Edited by Julian Zelizer. Boston: Houghton Mifflin, 2004, 411–27.

———. "Temperance Politics and Regional Political Culture: The Anti-Saloon League in Maryland and the South, 1907–1915." *Journal of Southern History* 1 (February 1997): 57–90.

Pickett, Deets, Clarence True Wilson and Ernest Daily Smith. *Cyclopedia of Temperance Prohibition and Public Morals*. New York: Methodist Book Concern, 1917.

Radoff, Morris L., ed. *The Old Line State: A History of Maryland*. Annapolis: Hall of Records Commission State of Maryland, 1971.

Rea, Evan. "The Prohibition Era in Baltimore." Master's thesis, University of Maryland, 2005.

Ritchie, Donald. *Electing FDR: The New Deal Campaign of 1932*. Lawrence: University Press of Kansas, 2007.

Rose, Kenneth D. *American Women & the Repeal of Prohibition*. New York: New York University Press, 1996.

Rose, Lou. "Social Attitudes toward Prohibition: A Calvert County Example." *Calvert County Historical Society News* 2 (January 1983): 1–2.

Rothbard, Murray. "World War One as Fulfillment: Power and the Intellectuals." *Journal of Libertarian Studies* 9, no. 1 (Winter 1989): 81–125.

Rumbarger, John J. *Profits, Power, and Prohibition: Alcohol Reform and the Industrializing of America, 1800–1930*. Albany: State University of New York Press, 1989.

Sanchez, Tanya Marie. "The Feminine Side of Bootlegging Louisiana History." *Journal of the Louisiana Historical Association* 41, no. 4 (Autumn 2000): 403–33.

Schaller, Thomas F. "Democracy at Rest: Strategic Ratification of the Twenty-First Amendment." *Publius* 28, no. 2 (1998): 81–97.

———. "Institutional Design, Institutional Choice, and the Case of Prohibition-Repeal." PhD diss., University of North Carolina–Chapel Hill, 1997.

Scharf, J. Thomas. *The Chronicles of Baltimore: Being a Complete History of "Baltimore Town" and Baltimore City from the Earliest Period to the Present Time.* Westminster, MD: Heritage Books, 1989.

Schoeller, Arne L. "American Beer on the Rocks." *Zeniada Magazine* (Spring 1986): 24–25.

Silberman, Lauren R. *Wicked Baltimore: Charm City Sin and Scandal.* Charleston, SC: The History Press, 2011.

Silva, Ruth C. *Rum, Religion, and Votes: 1928 Re-Examined.* University Park, PA, 1962.

Sinclair, Andrew. *Era of Excess: A Social History of the Prohibition Movement.* New York: Harper & Row, 1962.

Skotnes, Andor. "The Communist Party, Anti-Racism, and the Freedom Movement in Baltimore, 1930–1934." *Science and Society Journal* (1997). https://www.jstor.org/stable/40403552?seq=1#page_scan_tab_contents.

Stenerson, Douglas C. "The 'Forgotten Man' of H.L. Mencken." *American Quarterly*, no. 4 (Winter 1966): 686–96.

Stockett, Letitia. *A Not Too Serious History of Baltimore.* Reprint, Baltimore, MD: Johns Hopkins University Press, 1997.

Sullivan, Jack. "The Supremes and Whiskey by Mail: Then and Now." *Bottles and Extras* (Fall 2005): 1–7.

Szymanski, Ann Marie E. "Dry Compulsions: Prohibition and the Creation of State-Level Enforcement Agencies." *Journal of Policy History* 11, no. 2 (1999): 115–46.

———. *Pathways to Prohibition: Radicals, Moderates, and Social Movement Outcomes.* Durham, NC: Duke University Press, 2003.

Timberlake, James H. *Prohibition and the Progressive Movement, 1900–1920.* Cambridge, MA: Harvard University Press, 1963.

Turpeau, David DeWitt, Sr. *Up from the Cane Brakes: An Autobiography.* N.p.: self-published, n.d.

Vail, Keith Robert. "Anti-Saloon League of Maryland." Master's thesis, Salisbury State College, 1985.

Walsh, Michael T. "The Prohibition Era in Baltimore and Maryland, 1918–1933." Master's thesis, University of Maryland, May 2002.

———. "Wet and Dry in the Land of Pleasant Living: The National Policy of Prohibition." PhD diss., ProQuest, University of Maryland, 2012.

Walsh, Richard, and William Lloyd Fox, eds. *Maryland: A History, 1632–1974.* Baltimore: Maryland Historical Society, 1974.

Walton, Hanes, Jr., and James E. Taylor. "Blacks and the Southern Prohibition Movement." *Phylon* 32, no. 3 (Third Quarter 1971): 247–59.

Warburton, Clark. *The Economic Results of Prohibition.* New York, 1932.

Whitaker, M.C. "Industrial Alcohol and Its Relation to Prohibition Enforcement from the Manufacturer's Standpoint." *Journal of Industrial and Engineering Chemistry* (July 1921): 647.

White, Frank F., Jr. *The Governors of Maryland, 1777–1970.* Annapolis, MD: Hall of Records Commission, 1970.

Woman's Christian Temperance Union. "History." https://www.wctu.org/history.html.

INDEX

ABOUT THE AUTHOR

Michael Walsh, a native of Baltimore, Maryland, is a historian who specializes in both twentieth-century U.S. history and local history. Michael majored in history and received his undergraduate degree from Loyola University Maryland. He obtained a master's degree in historical studies at University of Maryland Baltimore County

Photo by Jennifer Walsh.

(UMBC) and subsequently earned his PhD at UMBC in public policy with a concentration in policy history.

Michael currently teaches U.S. History I as an adjunct history professor at the Community College of Baltimore County and is also a grants and contracts manager and training coordinator at UMBC. You can be certain to find him at many events and live music venues throughout Maryland as he rumbles on his bass guitar and provides vocals with two regional rock-and-roll bands, Whisky Train and The Agitators. Michael currently resides with his wife, Jennifer; daughter, Elizabeth; and pet Australian shepherd, Mugsy, in the Parkville community in Baltimore County.